Shaking Scripture

Grasping More of God's Word

Rev. Mark Manning

TRI-PILLAR
PUBLISHING

SHAKING SCRIPTURE

Tri-Pillar Publishing
Anaheim Hills, California
Website: www.TriPillarPublishing.com
e-mail: tripillarpublishing@cox.net

International Standard Book Number --13:   978-0-9818923-5-1

International Standard Book Number --10:   0-9818923-5-3

Library of Congress Catalog Card Number: 2012934268

First edition, March, 2012

Printed in the United States of America

Contents

Contents (continued)

*To my kids, who bring such joy to my life,
and to Heather, my partner in everything.*

Acknowledgments

There are many people who have had a hand in shaping this book, and for whom I have tremendous respect and gratitude. To all of you, I give my most sincere thanks!

To the members of Searchlight Ministries: Without all of your encouragement to vigorously study the Bible, I would have never written this book. You allowed me the freedom to spend so much time on sermon preparation. I owe you all a tremendous debt of love for allowing me to share all that God had given to me.

To the members of St. Paul's Lutheran Church: Thank you for the opportunity to share the Scriptures with you. You took a chance with me as we began in the book of Hosea... not an easy book to start off with. But God taught us a lot and I look forward to so much more ministry together as your pastor.

To Pastor Ron Martin: It is a joy to be back working with you again. You have been a great supporter throughout the years and I am enjoying the ministry we collaborate on. Blessings to you, your family, and your future!

To John Herrick: Thank you for your friendship. Your support of me and the church has allowed me the chance to write this book. Your initial edits were so insightful and helped me tremendously to improve as a writer. I am in awe of your skills as an author and I pray for God's richest blessings on all your future work.

To Diane Gihring: You have always supported me as a minister and a friend. Thanks for constantly pushing me to pursue this book, even when there were times I wanted to give up. And you continued that support by graciously providing me with so many corrections to my material. Thank you so much!

To Rich Manning: Hyaaaa! Your work as an editor is so appreciated. I strive to be as talented as you are as a professional writer. But alas, God has given you so much natural ability to craft ideas as a master wordsmith. Your friendship is invaluable and I am thankful that God had our paths cross so many years ago!

To Pastor Bob Dargatz: You are a wise man, and I was thrilled when you agreed to check over much of my material to make sure doctrinal issues are sound and that foreign language questions could be answered. You have given above and beyond what I asked for, and it made all the difference in the world.

To Andy Dibble: I cannot even imagine how many hours you put in to make sure that all the little details are perfect. What an incredible talent you have for editing. It has been wonderful working with you on this labor of love.

To Peter Dibble: You are a talented young man. Thank you for taking what was in my head and being able to re-create it for the cover of the book. It exceeded my expectations and your ability to make all the right changes made a huge overall impact. Thanks!

To Josephine Dibble: Thank you for taking a chance on a new author. I know you broke so many of your rules by editing this book. The amount of time you've spent and your incredible editing abilities leave me speechless. Thank you so much. I look forward to many more books with Tri-Pillar Publishing.

To Heather Manning: Words cannot express the depth of my love for you and the boys. You've supported me as a husband, father, author, pastor, and friend. Without you, this book would have never happened. Thanks for all the work on the reflective questions, and thanks for never giving up on me!

To God: Lord, I thank You for everything. I surrender this book to You for Your purposes. May You use it to bring people into a relationship with You and to strengthen the faith of Your children. I am Your humble servant. To You be all the glory. Amen!

Foreword

Growing up, I knew where in the house I could find my mother. She spent every spare moment sitting at the kitchen table with her nose in the Bible. I didn't understand why but figured it was the Christian thing to do. I didn't read the Bible regularly until age 14. The only reason I made the commitment was because my pastor promised us if we would read the Bible daily, we would find new meaning. So I took to reading the Bible regularly. Each day, it felt like I had accomplished something honorable, but I'll admit, I didn't get much out of it then. Frankly, I found it mundane, got little out of it, and made it my daily goal to get the ordeal over with. But year after year, I pressed on.

Then I turned 18, went away to college, and God taught me He could become your best friend.

As a freshman in college, I was a Christian, but I reached a point where I grew desperate to know God better. He provided some additional Bible teaching that suited my needs. I began to dive into His Word with greater hunger. And at 18 years old, I discovered that God has filled the Bible with treasures. As I read the pages and learned how the verses applied to everyday life, I spent a year saturated in God's Word. You see, I learned that the words in the Bible aren't simply printed words. They aren't a two-dimensional product, mere ink on paper. God revealed to me something He has revealed to generations of seekers: No matter how many times you have read a particular verse, God can show you something you've never before seen in it or provide insight into why He put those words in that context. This became perhaps my favorite facet of Scripture. The printed words don't possess height and width – they also contain an infinite depth. That year, I discovered the Bible is, in fact, three-dimensional.

It's easy for us to look at the people in Bible passages as larger-than-life. We regard them as faith heroes but risk overlooking the obvious: They were parents concerned for their kids, citizens who paid taxes, individuals who got tired of waiting and, with God's help, took matters into their own hands. The Apostle Paul followed God's call on his life – yet he worked a side job as a tentmaker to pay his bills. And as Abraham believed God, he had to struggle with God's promise versus his circumstances that appeared to be contrary. I doubt Abraham knew he would end up in the Scriptures; I think he was just a man on life's journey with God.

When we dig down into who these people were and the struggles they endured, we discover they were simply people like us with core issues like ours. They were real individuals with real needs, for whom the Lord provided real answers – even if it took a miracle.

As we read how God walked beside them and intervened on their behalf, we can rest assured that God will walk beside *us* and intervene on *our* behalf. If the Lord did it for them, we can be confident He will do it for us today because, in meeting the needs of people in the Bible, He revealed aspects of His nature: He is the Lord our healer ... our provider ... our protector ... our friend. And most amazing of all, when we were lost and without hope, He became the Lord our Savior, Jesus Christ.

His nature never changes. He was God for those in the Bible. He will continue to be God for us – forever.

As a novelist, I thrive on characters. I want to know who they are: their personalities, the light and dark corners of their backgrounds, the choices and ramifications that shape who they are. More than the plot itself, I love to see how characters respond to the circumstances they face. I love to walk with them, step-by-step, and record not only what they do and say, but *why* they do and say those things. This enables readers to relate to those characters, to recognize in them an inkling of themselves. I pray God will use my characters to resonate with the hearts of readers.

From time to time, someone will select individuals in the Bible, walk through a similar process as a novelist does, with the same goal in mind.

In *Shaking Scripture*, Rev. Mark Manning has crafted a landscape of insight into human nature, its limitations, and its desperate need for a God who meets practical needs. By capturing Biblical individuals at their most vulnerable and most comical, we become acquainted with people we've heard much about and discover how closely they resemble you and me. Manning transports these individuals to a 21st century context to reveal how human beings – and the Lord Himself – remain remarkably constant. His book both touched my heart and made me laugh aloud.

Straightforward and honest, engaging and comical, *Shaking Scripture* is a must-read.

John Herrick
Author of *From the Dead* and *The Landing*

Introduction

I have come to love the Bible. I know that sounds like a cliché that so many pastors have thrown around. But, for me, it has become a wonderful passion that has lasted for over ten years now, without any signs of slowing down.

I think most Christians would also say that they love the Bible. They have been taught through the years that this document is where we turn to discover the truth about God, Jesus Christ, humanity, and salvation. But for many, it seems that their love for the Bible goes only so far as saying it. Very little in their life demonstrates that the Scriptures are an important part of their belief system.

Churches will often have the study of God's Word as a core value in their mission plan. It just sounds good. But many congregations have very little knowledge about the contents of The Book. For example, for many pastors there is a tendency to prefer topical sermon series that tackle subjects they feel more easily apply to their parishioners. *Five Steps to Financial Freedom, Ten Lessons on Having a Better Marriage*, and similar themes have replaced verse-by-verse preaching through books of the Bible. This and similar shortcuts have contributed to a widespread ignorance that permeates the clergy and laity alike, and that has led to what I view as a general sense of Biblical illiteracy in Christianity today.

I remember being caught up in the allure of preaching topical sermon series. I believed that the Bible was boring and it needed a little "spicing up" so that my parishioners could grow in their faith in a better way. Little did I know that I was undermining the value of Scripture by thinking that my cleverness could outdo the magnificent material of those 66 books. Luther aptly described the state I was in when he wrote:

> *The neglect of Scripture, even by spiritual leaders, is one of the greatest evils in the world. Everything else, arts or literature, is pursued and practiced day and night, and there is no end of labor and effort; but Holy Scripture is neglected as though there were no need of it. Those who condescend to read it want to absorb everything at once. There has never been an art or a book on earth that everyone has so quickly mastered as the Holy Scriptures. But its words are not, as some think, mere literature; they are words of life, intended not for speculation and fancy but for life and action. But why complain? No one pays any attention to our lament. May Christ our Lord help us by His Spirit to love and honor His holy Word with all our hearts. Amen* (LW 14:46).

Though this was the state I was in, God had plans for me to rediscover His Word in a way I never thought possible, and to instill within me a passion and drive to learn as much as I can regarding all He has spoken to us.

In 1998, I was privileged to be involved in the launching of a new church called Searchlight Ministries. There were seven of us who envisioned a congregation without the traditional baggage of history that so often stifles creativity and freedom. The very first thing I preached at Searchlight was a topical sermon series. Through the next couple of years, I went back and forth from preaching a topical sermon series to teaching through a book of the Bible. Along the way, I started loving the research and the material I was discovering while studying Scripture. The words on the pages started coming alive for me like never before. I began to understand what Paul meant when he wrote: **"For the word of God is alive and active. Sharper than any double-edged sword, it penetrates even to dividing soul and spirit, joints and marrow; it judges the thoughts and attitudes of the heart"** (Hebrews 4:12).

I started craving the time I set aside to study Scripture. I especially enjoyed learning more about the books of the Old Testament. Like most Christians, I had a general idea of some of the stories within that first section of Scripture, but I had no idea the depth that the Old Testament had.

Things continued to change with regard to my preaching when we chose to go through the book of Genesis. I was doing something that I had vowed never to do. I had been taught that 8-10 weeks is about all that a congregation can handle when it comes to a sermon series. Up until that point, I had stuck mainly to smaller books of the Bible that I could finish in that amount of time. I wasn't sure what I was going to do with a 50-chapter book! When we dove in, it was so wonderful being able to go back to the beginning of Scripture and read some rather familiar material. But as I began this series, I tried covering three chapters a week. I finally had some parishioners come and ask me to slow down. They shared that we were skimming over way too much material, and that they wanted to learn all they could from this important book. I told them that if I slowed down, it might take us a whole *year* to get through Genesis. Their response? *"Who cares how long it takes! We just want to learn Scripture!"* From that point on, I progressed through the book of Genesis much more slowly. It was challenging at times, covering material that is rather sordid in parts, and trying to understand cultures vastly different from our own. But by the end, I felt rather confident that we had mastered the main concepts and had gotten quite a lot out of our study.

I did a quick poll of the congregation to see what they would like to cover next. Excitement had built up so much by that point that they told me we should continue on into the book of Exodus. From that point on, I have never worried about how long it will take to cover a book, or if the Old Testament has enough material for me to preach on. I trust that God's Word is sufficient and that my calling is to study, learn, and grow as a pastor, and then share my insights the next week with the congregation. During this time, my faith and knowledge have grown tremendously, and I know those who are regular in their attendance can say the same.

During the decade that followed, I had the privilege of studying, in depth, 43% of the Bible. I know there is a long way to go, but I have no plans of slowing down any time soon. I have come to appreciate the language, the description, and the beauty of all the different parts of the Bible.

I pray that *Shaking Scripture* will help you grasp just how exciting the Bible can be, as the stories come to life. Along with that, I hope that your faith will also come alive. The words of Psalm 1:1-3 sum this up perfectly:

> **Blessed is the one who does not walk in step with the wicked or stand in the way that sinners take or sit in the company of mockers, but whose delight is in the law of the LORD, and who meditates on his law day and night. That person is like a tree planted by streams of water, which yields its fruit in season and whose leaf does not wither – whatever they do prospers.**

May God richly bless you as you study the material in this book, and put what you learn into practice. Together, we can be "Shaking Scripture" and flourishing as followers of God!

A Note about the *For Further Reflection* Section

As I set out on this adventure of *Shaking Scripture*, it became apparent that reflective questions would be a valuable part of the book. Many people want to delve a little deeper and ask a few more questions. Small group leaders are always looking for material that examines Scripture more closely, and would love to have something that they can use with a group right away. This book is also designed for those who are more interested in self-study. We have designed the *For Further Reflection* section to allow it to be used in as many applications as possible. Many people enjoy reading an entire devotion and then going back to answer reflective questions on the material they've just read. Others may want to use this in a small group, where the people gathered will start and stop the discussion as they are reading through the devotion. With that in mind, we designed this section to help you.

As you read through the devotions, in the outside margin there are numbered Bible symbols (such as given in the margin here). The number corresponds to a question in the *For Further Reflection* section at the end of the book. If you wish, you can stop your reading at that point and turn to the end to read and answer that question. But if you prefer, you can simply gloss over the symbols and read the devotion in its entirety, and then turn to the reflective questions to read and answer all of them together. I am indebted to my wife who not only came up with this idea but also supplied the questions. She is an amazing leader, teacher, and educator, and I am grateful that she was a part of this project.

The Greatest Bible Study Never Recorded

Now that same day two of them were going to a village called Emmaus, about seven miles from Jerusalem. They were talking with each other about everything that had happened. As they talked and discussed these things with each other, Jesus himself came up and walked along with them; but they were kept from recognizing him.

He asked them, "What are you discussing together as you walk along?"

They stood still, their faces downcast. One of them, named Cleopas, asked him, "Are you the only one visiting Jerusalem who does not know the things that have happened there in these days?"

"What things?" he asked.

"About Jesus of Nazareth," they replied. "He was a prophet, powerful in word and deed before God and all the people. The chief priests and our rulers handed him over to be sentenced to death, and they crucified him; but we had hoped that he was the one who was going to redeem Israel. And what is more, it is the third day since all this took place. In addition, some of our women amazed us. They went to the tomb early this morning but didn't find his body. They came and told us that they had seen a vision of angels, who said he was alive. Then some of our companions went to the tomb and found it just as the women had said, but they did not see Jesus."

He said to them, "How foolish you are, and how slow to believe all that the prophets have spoken! Did not the Messiah have to suffer these things and then enter his glory?" And beginning with Moses and all the Prophets, he explained to them what was said in all the Scriptures concerning himself.

As they approached the village to which they were going, Jesus continued on as if he were going farther. But they urged him strongly, "Stay with us, for it is nearly evening; the day is almost over." So he went in to stay with them.

When he was at the table with them, he took bread, gave thanks, broke it and began to give it to them. Then their eyes were opened and they recognized him, and he disappeared from their sight. They asked each other, "Were not our hearts burning within us while he talked with us on the road and opened the Scriptures to us?"

They got up and returned at once to Jerusalem. There they found the Eleven and those with them, assembled together and saying, "It is true! The Lord has risen and has appeared to Simon." Then the two told what had happened on the way, and how Jesus was recognized by them when he broke the bread.

(Luke 24:13-35)

Quick show of hands: Who would like to attend a two-hour-long Bible study exclusively studying the Old Testament? Anyone?

I can hear the crickets chirping.

What if I told you that the Old Testament is actually exciting, informative, and amazingly relevant to your life – right here, right now? You might be thinking that I am absolutely crazy at this point. But I believe you will discover this truth for yourself, if you are willing to take a chance on those first 39 books of the Bible. One of the reasons I have come to this conclusion is because of the story recounted for us above, from Luke 24.

Luke is the only person to record this story in detail, so I tip my hat to the good doctor for giving us this incredible account that helps give us an even deeper appreciation for the Word of God. It is this story that truly opened my eyes to the depth, richness, and fullness of Scripture, particularly the Old Testament. Upon further study, I am confident you will have the same experience.

This episode immediately follows *the* greatest story ever recorded – the account of Jesus Christ and His resurrection. Nothing can compare to the world-changing events that took place on that first Easter morning. Jesus had told His disciples that He would die, but promised that He would come back from the dead three days later. And that is exactly what happened! The resurrection of Jesus has been and always will be the cornerstone of the Christian faith (1 Corinthians 15). The claims of Jesus become validated as He begins to show Himself to some of the believers. His first post-resurrection appearance is to several women who were devoted followers (Matthew 28:5-9). One of those women, Mary Magdalene, encounters Him in the garden by the tomb (John 20:14-18). And now, later that same day on a road leaving Jerusalem, Jesus joins up with a pair of believers on their journey to Emmaus.

Little is known about our two travelers. In verse 18, we discover that one of them is named Cleopas. The other person's name and personal details remain a mystery to us. Most pastors and commentators refer to them as disciples even though the narrative never specifically calls them this. From the information available, we can safely deduce that they are very close followers of Jesus. They know Him and are aware of the details surrounding His crucifixion. They were in Jerusalem when it happened, and could bear witness to the widespread knowledge of the event. They even know that Peter and John ran to the tomb after the women had discovered it was empty. Later on in our story, we learn that these two return to Jerusalem and have direct access to the disciples. It isn't until verse 33 that we learn for certain that neither of these two is counted among the Eleven. (Remember that Judas is already dead and Matthias hasn't been chosen as his replacement quite yet.) And with the events that directly follow this story, apparently they are present with the disciples the first time Jesus miraculously appears and gives a physical demonstration of His resurrection to this large of a group. It is for these reasons that I will refer to these two men as *disciples* for the remainder of this devotion.

So Cleopas and his companion are on their way out of Jerusalem and headed to a town seven miles away. We aren't too sure why they are leaving. Perhaps they are returning home after an extended stay in Jerusalem. Although they are privy to the information that Jesus might have risen from the dead, they aren't sticking around to see if the reports are true. There appears to be a depressed resignation among these two that perhaps Jesus was not who He claimed to be, and that they had been following a false Messiah.

As they walk along the road, they are talking about the events of the previous days. Confused and disappointed, they are still trying to process all that has taken place. In verse 15, our text says that they **"discussed these things with each other."** However, I don't believe they are merely *discussing* these events; they seem to be arguing about them. The Greek word used here is συζητεῖν (*suzhtein*), which carries the connotation of arguing or debating. The exact same word is found in Mark 9:14 and 16, Luke 22:23, Acts 6:9, and Acts 9:29. From these particular verses, we can infer that Cleopas and his companion are not merely engaging in a casual chat here. It is more like a debate. Although the text is silent about the topic they are debating, I wouldn't be surprised if it involved the resurrection, and the claims of the women and disciples regarding the empty tomb.

Excellent! This concept excites me! I firmly believe that we need more debate among Christians. Now, let me clarify something. When I say "debate," I'm not referring to bitter arguments or fighting. I'm not advocating divisiveness and angry verbal attacks, consisting of yelling matches where true dialogue is absent. I'm talking about a genuine debate that allows people to have an effective back-and-forth discussion and a sharing of alternative viewpoints that will stretch and grow their faith.

I remember a time when I was leading a group through an adult instruction class that was designed to cover the major topics of Christianity. One night, we were debating the concept of infant baptism and the meaning behind the sacrament of Holy Communion. I had shared my conclusions based on my study of the Scriptures. Many people were questioning me and bringing up other Scripture passages along with other Christian viewpoints. It was a spirited discussion with plenty of dialogue, and various opinions were exchanged. I thoroughly enjoyed it! By the end of the class, I believe we all had grown in our faith and in our understanding of why we hold certain beliefs in our particular denomination. But I also remember one quiet couple who were sitting in the back corner of the room. They were silent throughout the entire class, and not once did they enter into the conversation with their thoughts or ideas. After the class was over for the evening, I approached them and asked if everything was okay. I mentioned that I hadn't heard them share any of their own viewpoints, and that I hoped they had still learned something from the discussions. They meekly explained that they used to be Catholic, and they had been told never to argue with the pastor. I was amazed! I regularly encourage my congregation to immerse themselves in the Word daily, and always to feel comfortable disagreeing with me if they have grounds to do so. Remember that pastors and other church leaders are human and can make mistakes from time to time. On occasion, during a sermon or Bible class, I have said something from a more limited point of view, only to be corrected by sound, solid Biblical evidence. I always appreciate and welcome the opportunity to grow and learn if I am mistaken. Even Peter had to be corrected at one point early in the church's history (Galatians 2:11-14). How refreshing it would be to see more healthy debate inside the church today! This is a way we can help each other grow in our faith, and in the pursuit of God's Word and His truth. [2]

So in the midst of this discussion on the road to Emmaus, Jesus Christ Himself shows up! The text doesn't share the mechanics of exactly how He got there. I guess it is possible that He could have been power-walking down the road all the way from Jerusalem and simply caught up with them. But I would rather like to believe that He simply materialized on the road – and then fell into step beside them while they were engrossed in discussion. This is certainly possible, because when it is time for Him to leave, He doesn't walk away, but instantaneously disappears. (Now that is cool!)

One important detail given in the story is that they were kept from recognizing Jesus. This is a significant point because it presupposes that they *should* have recognized Him. They knew Him well enough that they should have been able to spot Him on sight. I am sure that they were with Him for many of His teachings, and possibly even present for His public execution. But when He appears beside them here on the road, they don't realize that it is Jesus. This seems to be a regular occurrence in His post-resurrection appearances, even with His closest friends. Earlier that same day, Mary Magdalene doesn't immediately recognize Jesus outside the tomb (John 20:14). When He appears to the Eleven back in Jerusalem later that night, they have doubts about His identity and speculate that He is a ghost (Luke 24:37). A week or so later, there is still some hesitation from the disciples when they meet up with Jesus by the Sea of Galilee (John 21:12). So why are His closest friends unable to "see" that this is Jesus? There are several possibilities as to why this might be the case.

We are not exactly sure what Jesus looks like in His resurrected body. Maybe there is a significant difference between the bodies we have on this earth and what we will have in heaven. I fantasize that my new physique will be free from the extra jiggle, having been replaced with bulging, perfect muscles. Perhaps the disciples didn't recognize Jesus because His resurrected appearance looked drastically different from the earthly one they had become so familiar with. ₃

A more likely scenario is that this was a simple, supernatural veiling by God. God's hand simply covered their eyes and they were kept from recognizing Jesus for who He really is. At this point in time, Jesus had a much greater purpose for keeping His identity hidden. If these two guys had recognized Him immediately, the excitement would have been overwhelming, and it's pretty safe to say that they probably would have missed out on the important teachings that Jesus wanted to share with them that day.

So as Cleopas and his companion are walking down the road, debating the events of the past few days, they realize that a fellow traveler is now walking alongside them. In typical Jesus fashion, He asks a question that He already knows the answer to: *"So ... whatcha all talkin' about?"*

Their response says it all. They come to a halt, standing there on the road with sad and gloomy faces. We can see just how deeply these guys are affected by Christ's death. Normally, if something is bothering us and someone tries to engage us in conversation, we can at least put on a brave face and act as if everything is fine. But not Cleopas and his friend; their emotions are out there for everyone to see.

These two disciples find it hard to believe that this inquiring fellow hasn't heard about all the things that have recently taken place. Now we can see just how widespread the news of Christ's death was in Jerusalem. Apparently, everyone knew about it. To paraphrase, they are saying to Him, *"Where have you been all this time? Under a rock somewhere?"*

(Well.... kinda... Not actually under it, but rather behind it.)

Jesus pretends to be clueless. I love it! *"What things are you referring to?"* The all-knowing Savior and Lord of the universe is asking these disciples to recount the events that

He had just gone through. I'd like to believe that Jesus had a little smile on His face when He asked that question.

They go on to give an account of the previous days. They explain that Jesus was a great prophet, powerful in speech and action, and: **"The chief priests and our rulers handed him over to be sentenced to death, and they crucified him; but we had hoped that he was the one who was going to redeem Israel"** (verses 20-21). Wow. They *had* hoped – past tense. Again, I believe we are dealing here with some depressed, struggling disciples trudging down the road. They have yet to realize that their hopes have truly been fulfilled – and that the greatest hope of all mankind is standing right there beside them!

I can relate to this situation as I reflect on all the times I have shared my shattered hopes and dreams with the Lord. Sometimes in my disappointment and pain, I find myself asking where He is and why I don't feel Him near. Looking back, I am completely convinced that He was actually right there beside me, closer than I could ever imagine. ₄

The two disciples continue sharing their story, explaining that it has now been three days since Jesus was put to death. Ah... so they *do* know that Jesus promised to come back to life! They must have been paying attention when Jesus said He was going to rise from the dead three days after He was killed. We know from Mark 8:31, 9:31, and 10:34 that Christ clearly stated that death would not be the end, and that He would come back from the grave. These disciples knew about this promise, but they are now wondering why it hadn't come true.

You see, they were skeptics. We can throw them into the "doubting Thomas" camp. They go on to share that several women found the tomb empty that morning, and angels told them that Jesus is alive. Two of their companions, Peter and John, had seen the empty tomb as well. But nobody had reported seeing Jesus Himself yet. If He is alive, where is He?

Without physical evidence to verify Jesus' resurrection, Cleopas and his friend are confused and unsure of what to believe at this point. Again, maybe this is what they were debating as they walked down the road. Perhaps one of them is hoping that the reports of the empty tomb and the declaration of the angels are true, and that Jesus actually is alive. But I can imagine the other saying, *"Yeah, but I want something more solid than a secondhand witness. I want to see Jesus with my own eyes."*

And then in comes the rebuke. Jesus scolds them for being slow to believe and for their failure to grasp *all* that the Old Testament had spoken of regarding the Messiah's mission, death, and resurrection.

I really can't fault these guys. After all, the Old Testament remains largely a mystery to most of us, even to this day. Sure, we may be able to point to some favorite stories or inspirational passages from that part of the Bible, but most people don't have much familiarity with this material. In fact, how many of us would be able to pinpoint texts that share the mission, death, and resurrection of the Messiah from the first 39 books alone? Perhaps Cleopas and his companion suffered from the same apathy toward the Old Testament as we generally have. They might have had certain portions memorized, but it seems as if they failed to study other sections. This "pick-and-choose" approach to Scripture often leads us to become even more discouraged and confused, particularly when it comes to the Old Testament. When we only focus on bits and pieces of the Bible and don't study

God's Word in its entirety, we are missing out on the big picture. ₅

I invite you to grab a Bible and open it up to the first chapter of Matthew, which is the beginning of the New Testament. Now take a look at how many pages come before it and after it. Notice the vastly different proportions between the Old Testament and the New Testament. When I did this, I was shocked to realize that most Christians aren't even familiar with what amounts to approximately three-quarters of the Bible. How careless and lazy we have become! It is this same carelessness that is evident in the two disciples on the road to Emmaus that elicits the rebuke and scolding of Jesus.

Thankfully, Jesus is not interested in simply chiding us, but rather He wants us to grow in knowledge and in faith. He doesn't stand there smugly in front of these two disciples, like some righteous know-it-all. Instead, **"beginning with Moses and all the Prophets, he explained to them what was said in all the Scriptures concerning himself"** (Luke 24:27).

I must share my disappointment in how short this verse is. Oh, how I wish it were several hundred pages long! Undoubtedly, this is the greatest Bible study *never* recorded! Think about it for a moment. If He met up with this duo early on the road to Emmaus, then it is very possible that Jesus Christ led a two hour Bible study through the Old Testament, touching on all the passages that pertained to Him.

Now who here would love to have been a part of that study? I know that *I* would!

We often shudder when we imagine studying the Old Testament. We cringe at the thought of long genealogies, and seemingly endless details regarding mold and zits. These stories happened in a completely different time and place, and in a cultural setting that is quite foreign to our own experience. I'm afraid that if most churches offered a two hour Bible study through the Old Testament, the sign-up sheet would remain blank. I admit that the problem is likely a combination of our lack of desire to dig deeply into the Old Testament, along with a leader's inability to bring Scripture to life and remain sustained in that endeavor for any significant amount of time. This, unfortunately, is a very serious problem. Churches everywhere have the right to be instructed in ALL of Scripture, and clergy bear a responsibility to make the understanding of the Old Testament a higher priority in their sermon schedule. Yet, pastors are often hesitant to dive into the first three-quarters of the Bible because they feel ill-equipped in their knowledge and unable to spend the necessary time in study to properly lead an Old Testament lesson. Combined with the pushback they might receive from a church body that has no inclination to delve deeper into that material, the result is a Christian church that is largely ignorant of much of the Bible.

I know, I know. Your pastor is awesome. If *he* led the study, you would all certainly come. But let's be honest here. Most of us would rather spend two hours doing something completely different.

But Cleopas and his friend *loved* their Old Testament lesson! I am sure that Jesus started in Genesis, highlighting chapter 3 and the promise of someone who would come from Eve. Abraham's near sacrifice of his son Isaac (Genesis 22:1-18) would certainly have been on the list of topics covered. Pausing at Psalm 22 and Isaiah 53, Jesus would have shown these Scriptures as integral in the suffering of the Messiah. On and on they walked down the Emmaus road, listening to Jesus as He guided them through the text of the Old

Testament. Jesus had previously spoken on this topic when He was debating with some Jewish leaders bent on killing Him. Christ said to them: **"You study the Scriptures diligently because you think that in them you have eternal life. These are the very Scriptures that testify about me"** (John 5:39).

This is further highlighted in the book of Acts when we read of the Bereans. These folks carried with them a wisdom and determination to verify that everything Paul spoke was in harmony with the Old Testament: **"Now the Berean Jews were of more noble character than those in Thessalonica, for they received the message with great eagerness and examined the Scriptures every day to see if what Paul said was true"** (Acts 17:11).

Oh, how I wish we had the same attitude today! Throughout Scripture, we are given Christ and all of God's truth. So much knowledge and understanding can be found within those pages. And yet, we often treat the Old Testament with disdain, preferring to be fed in other ways. But I believe that when we study *all* of Scripture and dig in deeply, we will find Christ and all His glory. Jesus promises us that He is there! And when God opens up Scripture to us, we too will be burning with passion and desire to learn more!

Mile after mile, Jesus teaches and explains. When the group reaches the end of the journey, the two disciples start heading into Emmaus. Jesus, however, acts as if He is continuing on down the road. The two men insist that Jesus come stay with them – which is testimony that this must have been one of the most dynamic Bible studies ever given. If it had been a boring, dull, and inconsequential lesson, I am certain they would have simply smiled, waved, and happily said good-bye to this talkative stranger. (*"Hey Cleopas – thank goodness we finally ditched that guy! Did you notice that he never shut up the ENTIRE time?")* But no – these two want to hear *more!* They love it and beg Jesus to stay longer.

The Savior obliges. And at the dinner table, Jesus takes the bread, gives thanks, breaks it, and starts to give it to them. Wow! Jesus recreates the night of the Passover celebration – and it is in this very moment that they finally recognize who He is.

There are several theories as to how they figured it out. It could have been that the divine "veil" was simply lifted from their eyes at that moment. Maybe God was ready for them to see and understand His true identity. Or perhaps it was the fact that He was recreating the Passover, and these disciples knew of that night and what had taken place. But the majority of people seem to lean toward the idea that they finally realized it was Jesus because they saw His hands.

Jesus starts passing out the bread and they look down and catch a good view of His hands. The nail holes or scars must have been clearly visible. If it were me, I would have thought, *"Wow, that's interesting. Why does this guy have holes in his hands? He almost looks like he was recently crucified. But that can't be right. If you get crucified, there is no way to survive that form of execution. I mean, the only way that could happen is if this man was crucified and then was raised from the dead. Hmm. Who could that be? Wait a minute... IT'S JESUS!"*

And at the exact instant the two recognize it is Jesus, He disappears! Bravo! Could you imagine sitting there at the table one moment, and just when you figure out who your mystery dinner guest is, He vanishes right in front of you? The two wide-eyed disciples reflect on all that has happened over the past few hours. They look at each other and exclaim: **"Were not our hearts burning within us while he talked with us on the road and opened the Scriptures to us?"** (verse 32). What a great insight into what it was like to have Jesus as their small-group leader!

I believe that this same feeling of exhilaration from God's Word continues on today. God is still in the business of opening Scripture to us and having us receive inner excitement better than any acid reflux experience.

And it should do more than simply move our hearts; it should also move our feet. These gentlemen decide that it isn't enough for them to encounter Christ and then keep it to themselves. They needed to tell the others about it too! Despite the late hour, they make the perilous nighttime journey (another seven miles!) back to Jerusalem to speak to the Eleven. On arriving, they discover that Jesus has already appeared to them as well, verifying His resurrection. What joy and celebration! The two Emmaus travelers contribute their story and share the details of what has happened to them. What a party that must have been! Of course, whenever you get a group of people together talking about Jesus, you'd better watch out – He's going to show up. (And that is literally what happens here. While they are talking and sharing, Jesus appears again (Luke 24:36).)

These two disciples learned an incredible lesson that day – one they never forgot. Their hearts burned within them as they dug deep into Scripture (with Christ's help), and they could not contain themselves any longer. They were changed men!

Now it is time for you to make that same discovery. Don't be satisfied in missing out on the rest of the story. Find out if your church is currently offering a Bible study group that is exploring a book of the Old Testament. If not, maybe it is time to start one! Your local Christian bookstore has plenty of resources that will guide you through books of the Bible that you might otherwise be scared to read on your own. Your pastor can recommend some excellent study guides as well. Share with him your desire to cover more material in Scripture, particularly within the Old Testament. This is also a good opportunity to encourage him to teach and preach on these lesser-known books of the Bible. Do it with care and concern, knowing that he may be as terrified as you. Remember Cleopas and his companion; don't settle for a few small, familiar sections within those first 39 books. There is so much more to be discovered! Start chewing on that material and you will be surprised how well it fills you up!

You too can become excited about all that Christ has done. Your heart can "burn within you" as you study and learn Scripture. Search, seek, dig, ask, question, wrestle, and pray. It's time for us to be "SHAKING SCRIPTURE!"

We pray: Lord, how greatly we need Your instruction! When we turn the pages of our Bibles, we struggle to understand what we are reading. Forgive us, for we often give up too quickly and simply toss the book aside and turn to more entertaining endeavors. We pray for pastors and teachers in churches everywhere, that You may guide them to teach *all* of Your Word, and we praise You for those who continue to instruct us week after week. Open up the Scriptures so that we can learn, understand, and grow. Kindle a fire in our hearts that has us longing for more of Your Word every day. And then may that fire spread to our family, our friends, our church, and our world. Thank You for Jesus, our Savior and Teacher, in whose name we pray. Amen!

Sleeping with the Frogs

Then the LORD said to Moses, "Go to Pharaoh and say to him, 'this is what the LORD says: Let my people go, so that they may worship me. If you refuse to let them go, I will plague your whole country with frogs. The Nile will teem with frogs. They will come up into your palace and your bedroom and onto your bed, into the houses of your officials and on your people, and into your ovens and kneading troughs. The frogs will go up on you and your people and all your officials.'"

Then the LORD said to Moses, "Tell Aaron, 'Stretch out your hand with your staff over the streams and canals and ponds, and make frogs come up on the land of Egypt.'"

So Aaron stretched out his hand over the waters of Egypt, and the frogs came up and covered the land. But the magicians did the same things by their secret arts; they also made frogs come up on the land of Egypt.

Pharaoh summoned Moses and Aaron and said, "Pray to the LORD to take the frogs away from me and my people, and I will let your people go to offer sacrifices to the LORD."

Moses said to Pharaoh, "I leave to you the honor of setting the time for me to pray for you and your officials and your people that you and your houses may be rid of the frogs, except for those that remain in the Nile."

"Tomorrow," Pharaoh said.

Moses replied, "It will be as you say, so that you may know there is no one like the LORD our God. The frogs will leave you and your houses, your officials and your people; they will remain only in the Nile."

After Moses and Aaron left Pharaoh, Moses cried out to the LORD about the frogs he had brought on Pharaoh. And the LORD did what Moses asked. The frogs died in the houses, in the courtyards and in the fields. They were piled into heaps, and the land reeked of them. But when Pharaoh saw that there was relief, he hardened his heart and would not listen to Moses and Aaron, just as the LORD had said.

(Exodus 8:1-15)

I'm going to be honest here. I think Pharaoh is an idiot. In this section of Exodus, it is glaringly obvious how incapable this man is of using common, rational sense. He makes such illogical choices.

And so do we.

I would like to firmly establish the foolishness of this Egyptian leader. I want you to laugh at him and see the error of his ways. I want you to say to yourself, *"If I were Pharaoh, I would have done it differently."* In doing so, perhaps you can identify with this man, recognizing his clearly defined mistakes so that you will be able to identify the poor decisions you've made in your own life as well.

You might have heard of the ten plagues of Egypt before. The major players, Moses and Pharaoh, are pretty well-known. But there are other characters involved that make this story much more interesting. To help us in our understanding of the plagues, let's take a moment to backtrack and see what led up to these events.

The Israelites, at this time, were living under the protection of the Egyptians in an area called Goshen. For many years, they were quite comfortable as guests in the land. But as time went on, Egypt's attitude toward the Israelites began to change from hospitality to hostility. As the number of Israelites grew, the Egyptians became more and more oppressive. This growth eventually caused the Pharaoh to deem these neighbors a substantial threat. As a result, the people of God were enslaved by the Egyptians and stripped of all their rights and dignity. As years of oppression dragged on, the Israelites prayed and cried out to the LORD. God heard their pleas, and in His compassion, He finally sent a deliverer for His people – Moses. He had been raised by the Pharaoh's daughter and enjoyed high status as one of the royalty. But he had to flee ₁ into exile after defending one of his Jewish brothers from a cruel Egyptian taskmaster which resulted in the Egyptian's death. Although Moses might have been acquitted in our current-day judicial system, back in that time there was no chance that he would remain alive if he stuck around. The next 40 years of Moses' life were spent in training by God; He was preparing Moses to become the leader of the Israelite nation. When the time was right (which in this case was when Moses was at the ripe, old age of 80!) God spoke through a burning bush to Moses and shared with him the rescue plan for the Israelites. ₂

Moses was commanded by God to go and confront Pharaoh. Moses was to demand that Pharaoh release the people immediately, so they could make a three-day's journey into the wilderness to worship Yahweh at a particular mountain. Moses eventually followed these orders (after a LOT of convincing by God) and finally met face-to-face with

Pharaoh. As you can imagine, this was not received well by the Egyptian leader. He saw no need to liberate millions of slaves, and lose out on all the financial benefits of having such a large pool of cheap labor. He would need a little more "encouragement" beyond the request of an 80-year-old shepherd.

And that's when the plagues began. Starting in Exodus 7, God initiated a ten-step program designed to free His people. The hardness of Pharaoh's heart, however, caused pain and suffering for the Egyptian people whom he governed, including his own family. Too bad he wouldn't learn the all-important lesson here: God ultimately gets His way!

The first plague that was sent to help convince Pharaoh to cooperate with the LORD's command involved water being turned into blood (Exodus 7:14-24). It was a HUGE mess. All the waters in Egypt were affected. Blood was everywhere and not a drop of fresh water could be found in the land. And don't imagine for a moment that this was a case of "red tide" or red sediment being flushed into the main river. The Bible clearly states that this plague affected even the water being held in stone jars inside people's houses (Exodus 7:19)! This was a crisis that threatened the lives of everyone in the area. Blood would have been tracked throughout all the houses, including the royal palace. The water in storage would need to be dumped without any way of cleaning up afterwards. And in the heat of the desert, the stench that would have accompanied the coagulating blood must have been overwhelming. The fish in the Nile would be killed immediately, and soon other wild and domestic animals would drop dead from the lack of fresh water. But the Egyptian leader was one stubborn *hombre*. For several days, the water remained as blood, and Pharaoh remained resolute in his refusal to let the people go.

This brings us to the story of the second plague – frogs. At the beginning of chapter 8, Moses returns to Pharaoh, telling him once again, **"This is what the LORD says: 'Let my people go, so that they may worship me'"** (Exodus 8:1). Just as before, a consequence for disobedience is attached: **"If you refuse to let them go, I will plague your whole country with frogs"** (Exodus 8:2, NIV 1984).

Now, at first blush, the Pharaoh might have actually enjoyed the sound of this problem. The Egyptians relied on the flooding of the Nile River each year for irrigation purposes, and an abundance of frogs hopping around everywhere was considered a sign of good fortune. It meant that a good harvest year was in store for them. But God was about to teach the stubborn Pharaoh that too much of a good thing can be a bad thing. Moses warned Pharaoh that the land would be completely *covered* with frogs. This wasn't a case of frogs scattered here and there without being much of a nuisance. These frogs were going to be EVERYWHERE. They would be in the houses, the ovens, and the kneading troughs. And Pharaoh wouldn't be exempt from this plague either. They were going to be in the palace as well. They were even going to sleep in the beds!

You can almost hear an Egyptian husband saying to his wife, *"Hey, honey, can you put the roast in the oven? It's time to start thinking about dinner."* She yells back, *"Sure thing, babe!"* and heads to the kitchen to open the oven door. Her scream echoes through the house as out hop dozens of noisy, slippery frogs, leaving their filth and stench behind.

Or consider this: You're climbing into bed with your honey after a long day of work. You start to snuggle up to her when you realize she's a lot slimier than you remember. You ask her sweetly if she is trying out some sort of new lotion. It's then that the two of you realize that something is terribly wrong. You pull back the covers to see frogs lying in your sheets, getting nice and comfortable and making themselves at home. I don't know about you, but that would give me nightmares!

And since these amphibians were everywhere, the people would be at a loss for what to do. Back in those days, Egyptians revered the frog as a god that was responsible for granting good harvests and economic stability. And here, God is showing supreme power over this so-called god by providing thousands upon thousands of them. I can picture the LORD sitting on His throne, laughing at the irony of it all. Instead of being a "blessing" from a god, these frogs have been turned into a plague that is negatively affecting every aspect of people's lives. The land was completely covered with these creatures. Now also consider that there were actually penalties for killing a frog! I bet the Egyptians had a hard time taking a step without squishing one of them. How many people tripped and fell trying to avoid one of them, only to end up smashing ten more as they hit the ground? Can you imagine the incessant noise they'd make while you're trying to sleep, and the filth they would leave behind after relieving themselves on your kitchen table? *Disgusting!*

And in verse 7, we head back into Pharaoh's court and are introduced to some very powerful men, serving as advisors and wielding a tremendous amount of influence over the leader. The text of Exodus doesn't list their names or how many there were. However, we do have Talmudic texts along with the testimony of 2 Timothy 3:8 that lead us to believe that there were two conjurers who seemed to be in charge, by the name of Jannes and Jambres. I like to affectionately call them Dumb and Dumber.

Whoever hired these guys to serve at Pharaoh's side must have been pretty desperate. Maybe they had stellar resumes, or perhaps they put on a great magic show. It also wouldn't surprise me if they had demonic powers backing them up, because what these guys were able (and NOT able) to do makes it clear that God was not supplying their abilities. These court magicians had been hanging around the palace since the beginning of the showdown between Moses and Pharaoh. Most recently, they were present at the onset of the first plague, when Moses had struck the Nile River and God turned it all to blood. In fact, one of the reasons Pharaoh wasn't impressed or persuaded by this event is that **"the Egyptian magicians did the same things by their secret arts"** (Exodus 7:22).

I admit that I have a few questions about the ability of the magicians to duplicate this transformation. First of all, since the text states that the water in all of Egypt had been turned into blood, where did these guys get their clean, plague-free water from? Call me skeptical, but I wouldn't be surprised if they merely claimed to have some clean water in a bucket, and before showing anyone the contents, they waved their magic wand, said a few words, and presto – *"Look, Pharaoh! Blood!"* I am not entirely convinced that anything magical took place here.

But if they did have the power to replicate this miracle, then what kind of magicians are these guys? Aren't they only making the problem worse? *"Hey Pharaoh! Look, we can make blood too – here you go!"* If I were Pharaoh, I would have been more impressed with them if they turned the blood *back into water*. Furthermore, if they actually did have fresh water, wouldn't it have been better to let everyone have a lifesaving drink rather than turn it into blood?

And now during the second plague, we find that Dumb and Dumber are at it again. Moses calls forth an innumerable amount of frogs to flood the land, and these clever magicians say, *"Hey... we can do that too!"* Again, I have my doubts. How did they prove that the frogs they supposedly called forth weren't already there? Did they say, *"Abracadabra!"* and then open a cupboard and out popped some frogs? If you really want to astonish me, guys, why don't you make them *disappear*? Why are you calling for even *more* frogs to show up?

You're fired!

As this second plague hits the land of Egypt, we can't help but wonder how long Pharaoh will be willing to endure such a pestilence. However, the text remains silent on the amount of time that passes, which infers that Pharaoh wasn't willing to wait it out like he had done with the plague of blood. This seemed to gross him out pretty badly. Or perhaps he suffered from ranidaphobia. Eventually, **"Pharaoh summoned Moses and Aaron and said, 'Pray to the LORD to take the frogs away from me and my people, and I will let your people go to offer sacrifices to the LORD'"** (Exodus 8:8).

Now we are getting somewhere! Pharaoh comes to his senses and begs Moses to intercede on his behalf to remove the plague. Moses even allows Pharaoh to choose the time when the frogs will depart (Exodus 8:9). At this point, you might be thinking to yourself, *"This is a no-brainer! Take the frogs away NOW!"* But nope, not this guy. I am completely stunned at the response.

"Tomorrow," Pharaoh says (Exodus 8:10).

Tomorrow? Really? You've got to be kidding me. You are actually asking to spend one more night with the frogs? What person, faced with such terrible circumstances, would deliberately choose to wait until tomorrow to find relief?

That would be me.

I admit that there have been many times in my life when I am faced with pain and suffering because of my sinful rebellion. God comes to me with a gracious offer: *"I can take away the pain, the guilt, the misery, the self-loathing. And I can do it right now."* And my response is, *"How about tomorrow?"* [4]

What is it that causes us to think that tomorrow would be a better time to get rid of the frogs in our lives? Why are we so comfortable sleeping with these amphibians? What compels us to keep these creatures around us for even one more day?

I often hear this lament from young adults attending college. They are filled with misery and emptiness. Their sexual "adventures" and empty beer bottles aren't enough to bring them happiness and satisfaction. They hop from bed to bed, sleeping with the frogs, trying to find meaning and purpose to their lives. But what do they have to show for it? Many wrestle with guilt their entire lives, while others suffer from depression. Along comes an offer of hope – *Jesus Christ has given Himself as a payment for all the sinful activities of your life. You may now experience true freedom and live for His glory in thankfulness and praise. All penalties are wiped clean.* Sounds like a good offer, right? But along with Pharaoh, they say, *"Tomorrow. Later. Not right now. Let me spend one more night with the frogs."*

I've seen many others faced with their sin. Maybe they've cheated on their spouse or struggle with pornography.

Perhaps they've submitted fraudulent income tax forms, or they repeatedly hurt others with lies and deceitful behavior. An offer is made to drag that sin into the light of God's grace and mercy, and to hear His promise of forgiveness and salvation. Stop carrying that burden around with you! Stop living with the frogs!

 "I can't do it. I'm stuck. Maybe later."

It seems that we humans can tolerate a lot of pain and suffering before turning our lives over to God. We go through so much needless misery trying to handle everything ourselves. What a shame. Don't wait any longer. Do you have a sin that needs to be confessed? Is there a person you need to talk to regarding something you've done? Are you wondering if there even *is* a God and if He cares about you? Are you tired of sleeping with the frogs?

Let's take care of the problem right now. Put this book down and pray. Lay your heart out before God, and talk to Him about the sin in your life. Seek out the person you've hurt, and confess your wrongdoing. Find relief from that plague called sin. The offer of freedom and forgiveness is yours for the taking.

Part of me understands why we hesitate. The story in Exodus 8 continues with what happened after the plague was lifted. We wonder what consequences we will have to face after we've decided to get rid of the frogs once and for all. We ask ourselves, *"What will our life be like when the frogs die?"* This fear became a reality for Pharaoh and his people as we learn: **"The frogs died in the houses, in the courtyards and in the fields. They were piled into heaps, and the land reeked of them"** (Exodus 8:13-14).

Make no mistake about it. Dead frogs stink. There will be times in our lives that the thought of cleaning up after the dead frogs is what keeps us living comfortably with the frogs in the first place.

We dread confessing our sin to our spouse, parents, children, or friends because we are scared of the consequences. How bad will it stink? Let's be honest. Many of our sins lead us into terrible troubles – messes that are hard to clean up – and we may try to convince ourselves that it's not worth it.

> *Will I lose my job if I confess to my boss that I've been stealing from the company? I can't afford the disgrace of being fired, and the financial consequences of being out of work. Maybe nobody needs to find out.*

> *Will my wife ever trust me again if I tell her that I've been having an affair? What if I lose my family? Is being honest worth the price I might have to pay? Lying seems much neater, and nobody gets hurt that way, right?*

Sometimes, our land reeks with the smell of dead frogs. Not surprisingly, we fear and dread the long and messy clean-up that lies ahead of us. But isn't it better than living with the frogs?

I would also like to encourage you not to attempt this task all by yourself. There are many resources available that will assist us in taking care of the stench and filth of our frogs. Pastors are always eager to help those who are struggling. Counselors are trained in giving concrete steps to clean up our lives. And though it may be tough to swallow your pride, your friends are there for a reason. You might be surprised at the kindness and wisdom of your closest confidants. Who knows? Maybe one of them has dealt with the very thing you are currently struggling with, providing you with someone who truly understands your situation and who can offer great advice on how to handle things. Put several of these beneficial relationships together, and you will build a tremendous support system to help you eradicate the frogs in your life.⁷

I make a promise to you that the anxiety you are feeling over confessing your sin is amplified by fear. Trust me – there will be a huge burden lifted from your life when you finally are rid of that sin. So often, I see people experience such great relief after they finally unload their burdens and take responsibility for what they have done. Yes, there might be pain and consequences for our actions. There will be times when we have to put on the Hazmat suit to deal with the cleanup. But living in the truth is always better than living day after day in deception and pain. Don't spend one more night with the frogs!⁸

I'd like to make one final point from this text. The misery of living with the frogs drove Pharaoh to seek help and ask for relief. And likewise, there are times when the suffering in our lives draws us into a closer relationship with God. Pain drives us back to His loving arms, and we cling to Him with all our might. But if we are honest, that pain is often what keeps us close to the Lord.

> **But when Pharaoh saw that there was relief, he hardened his heart and would not listen to Moses and Aaron, just as the LORD had said** (Exodus 8:15).

There is a huge temptation in our lives to completely forget about the plague of frogs after we've finally received relief from the suffering they caused. I've seen men who have cheated on their wives receive such incredible mercy and forgiveness from their spouses, only to return to infidelity **"as a dog returns to its vomit"** (Proverbs 26:11). How quickly they forget the pain and turmoil that comes from such actions! I've seen people return to church and have the most vibrant prayer life when their worlds have been turned upside down in chaos – only to have that fire quickly fade once they've been relieved of their suffering. I've watched families in financial distress become active participants in the life of the church in order to receive strength and support from the family of God – only to see them slide out the back door when their financial problems have been solved. ₉

Don't let your pain and problems drive you to God, only to have you crawl back in bed with the frogs later. Be aware that there will be a temptation to return to your sin. Find a person to whom you can be accountable. Journal your experiences in order to remind yourself of what life was like when you were trapped in this particular sin. Be vigilant about your prayer life. If you find yourself slipping, quickly confess to God (and others, if need be) before the problem gets out of hand again.

And by all means, don't spend one more night with the frogs.

> **I tell you, now is the time of God's favor, now is the day of salvation** (2 Corinthians 6:2). ₁₀

We pray: Father, God. We admit that we have sinful behaviors and addictions in our lives that we need to be rid of. We have held onto sin, guilt, and pain for far too long. Right now, we no longer want to spend one more night with the frogs. We cry out to You for relief, asking for Your great mercy in our lives. Take away the stench and filth from our sins, and wash us clean. We want freedom from the frogs and an abundant life in Your grace. Thank You for Your patience and kindness. In Jesus' name. Amen.

When You Don't Believe That Prayer Actually Works

It was about this time that King Herod arrested some who belonged to the church, intending to persecute them. He had James, the brother of John, put to death with the sword. When he saw that this met with approval among the Jews, he proceeded to seize Peter also. This happened during the Festival of Unleavened Bread. After arresting him, he put him in prison, handing him over to be guarded by four squads of four soldiers each. Herod intended to bring him out for public trial after the Passover.

So Peter was kept in prison, but the church was earnestly praying to God for him.

The night before Herod was to bring him to trial, Peter was sleeping between two soldiers, bound with two chains, and sentries stood guard at the entrance. Suddenly an angel of the Lord appeared and a light shone in the cell. He struck Peter on the side and woke him up. "Quick, get up!" he said, and the chains fell off Peter's wrists.

Then the angel said to him, "Put on your clothes and sandals." And Peter did so. "Wrap your cloak around you and follow me," the angel told him. Peter followed him out of the prison, but he had no idea that what the angel was doing was really happening; he thought he was seeing a vision. They passed the first and second guards and came to the iron gate leading to the city. It opened for them by itself, and they went through it. When they had walked the length of one street, suddenly the angel left him.

Then Peter came to himself and said, "Now I know without a doubt that the Lord has sent his angel and rescued me from Herod's clutches and from everything the Jewish people were hoping would happen."

When this had dawned on him, he went to the house of Mary the mother of John, also called Mark, where many people had gathered and were praying. Peter knocked at the outer entrance, and a servant named Rhoda came to answer the door. When she recognized Peter's voice, she was so overjoyed she ran back without opening it and exclaimed, "Peter is at the door!"

"You're out of your mind," they told her. When she kept insisting that it was so, they said, "It must be his angel."

But Peter kept on knocking, and when they opened the door and saw him, they were astonished. Peter motioned with his hand for them to be quiet and described how the Lord had brought him out of prison. "Tell James and the other brothers and sisters about this," he said, and then he left for another place.

In the morning, there was no small commotion among the soldiers as to what had become of Peter. After Herod had a thorough search made for him and did not find him, he cross-examined the guards and ordered that they be executed.

(Acts 12:1-19)

Have you ever prayed a prayer that you honestly didn't believe would be answered?

I am confident that most of the prayers that leave our mind or lips are offered up with the expectation that God may answer them in a way that we would view as favorable. For example, we pray for Aunt Jenny who has been diagnosed with cancer. Although we do not know the final outcome, we believe that God could conceivably heal her and that it is not out of the realm of possibility that a miracle can occur and she be instantly healed. Or perhaps we ask God to help us in our quest to find a job. We trust that He indeed hears our prayers, and if our request is in accordance with His will, He is going to lead us to gainful employment. Along with the knowledge that He *can*, we often believe that He *will* grant our request. Or maybe we pray for God to guide us in finding the right spouse to marry. We believe that God often reveals His plan for our lives in tangible ways. These are typical requests we have often prayed for.

But I'm talking about the other prayer requests – the ones we are almost certain God is not going to grant. I wouldn't go so far as to say that we don't believe that He can, but we have already decided that there is no reasonable chance of this miracle actually taking place. When our grandmother is failing from Alzheimer's, we may ask God to miraculously heal her, but at the same time we honestly don't think that He will. When deep depression suffocates your life, and you manage to whisper a desperate prayer for relief, you may still feel as if nothing will ever really change. When a loved one is at the point of death, you may find yourself pleading with God for just a few more months or even weeks of life. But it is hard to believe a miracle will happen when the doctors and nurses have made it clear that, from a medical standpoint, there is absolutely no hope remaining. Parents have been known to pray for their adult children who have fallen away from the Lord, hoping for something to change in them, but they have little faith that anything will ultimately be different because of their prayer. Spouses on the brink of divorce may utter a frantic prayer for their marriage, but the lawyers have already gotten involved – and at that point, why even bother believing that God will step in and save it.

I understand why we may come to believe such things about prayer. We simply take a look at what life has taught us and we become more "realistic" in our faith. Even pastors struggle with doubts when it comes to prayer. People in dire situations have asked me to pray for a miracle to happen, and there have been times when I have seriously doubted whether my prayers were really going to change anything. Sometimes the circumstances seem so overwhelmingly against all hope. Experience has shown us that we can often determine what an outcome will be in a tragic situation – and that miracles just don't happen for us, no matter how much we ask God for them. But since we are asked to pray, we do so, but with little or no confidence that it will be answered the way we hope.

At times like these, I often wonder about my trust in God. Of course I know that God can do anything He wants to do. I recall the words that Jesus spoke to His disciples in Matthew 19:26: **"With man this is impossible, but with God all things are possible."** I truly believe that we have an all-knowing, all-powerful Lord. Certainly, the One who created the entire universe and everything in it also has the power to heal my loved one's cancer or rescue a friend from the edge of destruction. And yet, as I look upon these situations from my humble, earthly, "realistic" standpoint, it still appears futile to even ask for such miracles. I am not proud to admit my weakness in this regard, and I shudder even writing it. But I suspect that many people have the same struggle. We would never say it aloud at a prayer meeting; we just pray obediently, even though our heart has distanced itself from any opportunity for the miraculous to happen. If this is how you have felt at times, then this devotion is just for you.

I believe the early church struggled with this same issue in the story given to us in Acts chapter 12.

The early Christian church at this time was under heavy persecution. In the beginning of this chapter, we read that King Herod was arresting those belonging to the church for the express purpose of persecuting them. This Herod was different from the Herod mentioned in Matthew 2, who was responsible for the slaughter of infants around the time of Christ's birth. He is also a different Herod than the one that Jesus appeared before while on trial, as described in Luke 23. This Herod was named Herod Agrippa, and he actually had a tie to the Jewish faith. In his zeal to keep the Jewish faith pure, he was actively attacking Christianity and its leaders. Because of Herod's political desire to remain in the good graces of the Jewish people – and his ruthlessness in dealing with anyone who would go against the Jewish faith – we read in verse 2 that **"He had James, the brother of John, put to death with the sword."**

In one short little verse, we read of such a tragic event. Let us not gloss over who was executed. James was one of the original twelve disciples and had become a pillar of faith within the early church. He was privileged to be a part of Jesus' inner circle of leaders, along with John and Peter, who were privy to many private moments of Christ. And shockingly, we read that he is now dead.

The Jewish people were absolutely overjoyed at what had happened. Their leadership was especially determined to put a halt to this start-up religion called *Christianity*. To them, Christ-followers were an abomination to the Lord and had absolutely no ties to the Jewish religion. So when one of the leaders of this new movement was executed, the Jewish people had cause for celebration.

Seeing the positive reaction from his Jewish constituency and wanting to remain in their good favor, Herod Agrippa pursued and captured yet another one of the main leaders of Christianity. Peter was now seized and thrown into jail. He was to suffer the same fate as his fellow disciple after standing trial. And every Christian knew what would happen next: Peter would be executed, and there wasn't anything that could be done to stop it.

Peter was placed under maximum security. The text specifically mentions that sixteen guards were on duty that night. Four guards were to be watching him at any given time, and there were twelve others standing by. Two of the guards were to be physically on the right and left side of Peter in his cell, chained to his wrists. The other two were stationed outside the door for added protection. There is no way that Peter would be able to escape. And since Herod is bent on killing this apostle, there is no possibility that his mind will be changed by some 11th hour appeal.

In the face of this impending crisis, the church has gathered together for prayer. One of their leaders had been incarcerated and is now awaiting the death penalty. It would have been natural for someone to suggest, *"We should pray for Peter."* So pray they did! Verse 5 shares that the church was "earnestly" praying to God for him.

The Greek word for "earnestly" (ἐκτενῶς, *ektenos*) is a very strong word. Its root word is only used a couple of times in

Scripture. It gives the connotation of straining. In Luke 22:44, we read of Jesus in the Garden of Gethsemane as the road to the cross was laid out before Him: **"And being in anguish, he (Jesus) prayed more *earnestly*, and his sweat was like drops of blood falling to the ground."** Wow, that is some serious prayer going on! Christ was straining and struggling so much in His prayers that it manifested itself in profuse sweating. The use of this same word in Acts 12:5 conveys that as the early church was gathered in prayer for Peter, they were taking their task very seriously and fervently praying on behalf of their leader.

[†]₂

I wish I knew *exactly* what they were praying for. Perhaps they were praying that God would provide Peter with strength in this time of trial. Maybe they were praying that he could be a witness to the people around him. I know I would have prayed that whatever happens in the situation, God would receive the glory. And I would like to think that these earnest prayers included a request for God to rescue this disciple from the clutches of Herod. It would be a natural thing for the church to pray for a divine "jailbreak" – because, you see, it actually happened before! Back in Acts chapter 5, the apostles had been thrown in jail for the night after the high priest and the Sadducees heard about all the healings they were performing, along with the sermons proclaiming Christ and His resurrection. While the details we are given in this story are a bit sparse compared to what we have here in chapter 12, we read, **"But during the night an angel of the Lord opened the doors of the jail and brought them out"** (Acts 5:19). Their release was followed by the angel's instructions for the apostles to return once again to the temple courts and continue preaching the message of salvation!

However, what happens next here in Acts 12 leads me to believe that even if the church *did* pray such a prayer, they didn't think that God was going to fulfill their request.

Now I want you to close your eyes for a moment and imagine Peter locked up in that dark, filthy jail, just hours before his trial and execution. You might picture him wide awake all night, pleading with God to **"take this cup from me"** according to His will, just as Jesus had prayed in the Garden of Gethsemane the night before His own trial and death (cf. Luke 22:42). Perhaps Peter is fearfully imagining the details of what is about to happen to him the next morning. Maybe his knees are pressed against the rough earthen floor as he anxiously prays for the survival of the church – and the strength of its believers – after his impending death.

But strangely enough, Peter is doing none of those things. Instead, he is fast asleep! That's right – the night before his trial and execution, Peter is snoozing soundly while being bound by chains between two soldiers standing guard over him. Instead of counting rats as they run across his feet, Peter is counting sheep. The stench from previous prisoners and the remains of rotten food aren't enough to keep Peter awake. The cold damp ground was still comfortable enough for him to get a good night's rest. What in the world gave Peter the ability to slumber deeply while his time on earth was quickly slipping away? There may be several reasons for this.

First, he may have simply trusted that even if he were to die that next day, he would soon be in heaven and in the presence of the Lord, and away from this earth and its painful trials and tribulations. Paul had a similar outlook on death, as he wrote in 2 Corinthians 5:8: **"We are confident, I say, and would prefer to be away from the body and at home with the Lord."** I have had the honor of ministering at the bedside of believers who were about to die. So often, they possess a sense of calm because they fully believe that they are about to enter into the most glorious existence of all time. I've even heard some of them express guilt over the fact that they are filled with such joy to be leaving this earth. Even though they are sorry that their death will cause pain for their loved ones, they see that the reality of heaven is very near. Peter might be experiencing that same sense of peace as he knows he will be entering into the glory of heaven within the next 24 hours.

Another explanation as to why Peter isn't lying awake with worry may be due to his past experience. As mentioned before, Peter has firsthand knowledge of what it is like to have an angel bust him out of prison. It is important that we draw strength from God's previous actions in our lives. Peter might be thinking, *"God has rescued me once, so He can do it again!"* [3]

Whatever the reason may be, Peter is sleeping like a baby while the church is earnestly praying. Suddenly, out of nowhere, an angel shows up with light shining all over the place. Angels are anything but subtle! You would think Peter would awaken from all that bright light. But apparently Peter is sleeping VERY soundly. The angel has no choice but to hit Peter in his side to rouse him! And apparently this isn't just a soft tap meant to gently wake a sleeping saint. I think he had to hit him hard. The original Greek word is πατασσω (*patasso*) and is used nine other times in Scripture. To help us understand this word a bit more, here are just a few passages where the same word is used:

> Matthew 26:31 – **Then Jesus told them, "This very night you will all fall away on account of me, for it is written: 'I will *strike* the shepherd, and the sheep of the flock will be scattered.'"**

Luke 22:49-50 – When Jesus' followers saw what was going to happen, they said, "Lord, should we *strike* with our swords?" And one of them struck the servant of the high priest, cutting off his right ear.

Acts 7:24 – He (Moses) saw one of them being mistreated by an Egyptian, so he went to his defense and avenged him by *killing (striking)* the Egyptian.

Acts 12:23 – Immediately, because Herod (the same Herod of our story) did not give praise to God, an angel of the Lord *struck* him down, and he was eaten by worms and died.

Get the picture? He didn't lean over and whisper softly, *"Wakey wakey, eggs and bakey."* He didn't tickle him with some of his angel feathers. Instead, this angel hauls off and whacks Peter to awaken him from his deep slumber. This gives a whole new meaning to the expression "touched by an angel!"

The shackles suddenly fall from Peter's wrists. I can just imagine Peter sitting there dumbfounded, unsure of what to do next. Because the night was cold and a half-naked man wandering the city streets would surely draw attention, the angel commands Peter to get dressed and **"follow me"** (verse 8). I guess there was no time for introductions or exchanging of pleasantries. You can sense the urgency in his voice with these simple instructions. And Peter simply obeys. Still groggy from his deep sleep, it is easy to imagine that he is somewhat disoriented. We learn from verse 9 that all along, Peter thinks that this is just a dream. But even in a dream, it probably would be best to listen to an angel giving you in-structions.

At this point, I have to wonder: What happened to all the guards who were there watching over Peter? Perhaps they were in a deep sleep, possibly brought on by God Himself. Or maybe they *were* awake, but a divine "veil" covered their eyes which prevented them from witnessing this miraculous escape. You see, back in those days, there were serious penalties for losing a prisoner. If you happened to be the guard on duty when a prisoner escaped, then you were either thrown into prison to finish out the punishment yourself, or you were simply put to death. (And in this particular case, the result would have been one and the same.) There was no room for error as a sentry! With their own lives on the line, these guards certainly would have done everything in their power to stop an escape attempt. However, it seems that they were somehow kept from realizing that this event even took place until the next morning (verses 18-19).

Now that Peter is properly clothed, the angel leads him out of the jail cell. Doors are unlocked and no resistance is encountered. The path to freedom is surely a whole lot easier with an angel escort! The irony in the whole situation is incredible. Herod had gone to great lengths to make sure that Peter was secure, but all of it was easily undone by God Himself. And in the dead of night, the pair makes its way out of the prison. Once outside, the cool, clean air fills Peter's lungs as the stench and filth of the prison is left behind.

They arrive at the massive iron gate that leads to the city. It miraculously opens by itself, and Peter, flanked by his heavenly friend, walks through without any issues. I can certainly understand why Peter was under the impression that this was all a dream. Chains falling off his wrists? Heavy doors opening automatically? This is a bit too easy! Not one guard notices them walking around, and no alarm is sounded that a prisoner is escaping. And then, after they walk the length of one street, POOF! The angel disappears.

This is when Peter REALLY woke up. The crisp night air has cleared his mind and senses, and he is now fully alert. Suddenly Peter finds himself alone, without an angel to guide his path any longer. It would be very disorienting and disconcerting to suddenly find himself out there in the empty streets in the middle of the night. Chills would be running down his spine as he starts to fully comprehend everything that has just happened to him – and that he is now a fugitive on the run, standing out in the open where he might be recognized.

His heart pounding, Peter's pace quickens as he heads toward the house where the church has gathered to pray. He isn't intending to stay very long, since his mere presence at that house would put everyone else in grave danger. In verse 17, we get the impression that his brief visit to the house is to encourage the people in their faith and to inform his fellow believers that he is alive and safe due to God's rescue. He desperately knocks on the door, trying not to wake up the neighbors or attract attention from anyone passing by on the street. He remembers the late hour and prays that his fellow church members have not all gone to bed or dispersed to their own homes for the night. He waits, but there is no answer. He knocks on the door again, this time a bit louder and with more urgency, begging to be let in.

Finally a servant girl named Rhoda comes to the door. She hears Peter's voice and suddenly realizes that it's him! Miraculously, their beloved leader is no longer in prison awaiting execution, but is actually standing right outside the door! In her excitement, she runs back into the room to share the news with all the prayer warriors – leaving poor Peter standing outside in the cold! Instead of being invited into the house, he is left out in the courtyard. I know if I were Peter, I would be pressing my face against the door, whispering as loudly as I dared, *"Come on guys! It's* me*! Let me in!* PLEASE!"* (In his article, "The Death of James and the Deliverance of Peter," author Bob Deffinbaugh cleverly notes that "the only door which failed to open that night was the door of Mary's house" (*Acts: Christ at Work Through His Church*; 1997, p. 203).) But Rhoda is overcome by her joy. She runs into the other room and blurts out to the prayer team, **"Peter is at the door!"** (verse 14).

It is what happens next in the story that causes me to speculate that those who were praying for Peter truly didn't believe that their prayers were going to be answered in the way that they hoped. If I had been sitting in that meeting and truly believed that my prayers could stir God to allow a man to be miraculously released from prison, I would have jumped to my feet excitedly and rushed to the door. In fact, you'd think that Rhoda's declaration would have been enough for every single person in that room to race eagerly to the door to see the answer to their prayers with their own eyes. But instead of being excited or even curious to see if Peter was really standing outside in the flesh, this group just assumes she is crazy, and they dismiss her comment as complete nonsense.

"'You're out of your mind,' they told her" (verse 15). (The King James Version phrases it even more humorously: **"Thou art mad"**!)

Not one of the prayer warriors at this all-night vigil even bothered to walk to the door to see if Rhoda's story was actually true. They just automatically assumed she was nuts. In fact, when Rhoda kept insisting that Peter was really standing outside, they go so far as to believe that it must be Peter's angel at the door. Back in those times, there was a popular belief that the guardian angels that are given to all believers (Hebrews 1:14, Matthew 18:10) could actually take on some of the physical characteristics of those they were sent to minister and protect. So the prayer group rationalizes that because Peter is still imprisoned, the person that Rhoda is conversing with outside the door must be Peter's angel. Think about that for a moment. Even after straining in prayer for hours deep into the night, pleading with God to spare Peter's life, they still find it easier to believe that it is Peter's angel that has shown up to knock on the door! These early Christians had seen the miraculous occur several times in their lives. The apostles in chapter 5 had been divinely rescued from jail once before. People were healed just by walking in Peter's shadow (cf. Acts 5:15). And most of them (if not all of them) were witnesses to a man rising from the dead after being in a tomb for three days! It is incredible how quickly our faith forgets all that God has done.

As I read this story, I am astonished by their disbelief in the midst of this incredible event. But then I pause to reflect on how many times in my own life I have been just as doubtful that my prayers would ever be answered in the way I wanted.

I stood at the bedside of my mom after she suffered a terrible heart attack. The doctors had shared with me that the heart damage that my mother had sustained was irreversible, and that medically speaking, there was nothing left for them to do. I remember kneeling beside her hospital bed, praying for a miracle. But I admit that even while I prayed that prayer, I honestly didn't expect anything to change. Of course, in my mind, I knew that God *could* accomplish it. But in my frail human condition, the medical evidence presented to me had convinced me that her death was inevitable – and that God wouldn't step in and change things. It just doesn't happen that way very often. And I am sure that Satan was right there beside me, whispering, *"Why even bother to pray? It isn't going to help at all. There is no hope."*

As I reflect on Peter's story, I can't help but wonder what my response would have been if the prayers I had lifted up for my mother had been granted – and she *had* been miraculously healed. If I were sitting at home and the hospital had called to say that my mom had suddenly made a full recovery and was doing fine, my first reaction would have been total disbelief. *"You must be confusing my mom with someone else,"* I would say. *"There is no way that my mother could have ever made it through!"*

I can understand why we have a hard time believing in miracles happening in our time. We just don't see them that often, or at least we don't perceive them. We have prayed so hard for our loved ones to be healed from diseases, or that cancer would disappear. More often than not, we've watched instead as their suffering increased and death claimed their lives, seemingly without as much as a whisper from God in response to our prayers. And as time goes on, a bitterness and resentment may begin to build up in our hearts about prayer. We wonder if it actually works, or if God is even listening. Maybe we question why some people are granted miracles and some are not. We don't know if it is worth the energy and breath it takes to bring our wants and needs to God. We are afraid to get our hopes up by praying for the unbelievable to happen.

In the midst of our skepticism, Satan comes along and whispers further words of condemnation in our ears. *"Wow.*

You don't actually believe that prayer works, do you? That's pathetic. Your faith is so weak. In fact, God can't do anything good in your life because you don't even have enough faith to ask anymore. You must be a pretty lousy Christian." There have been times in my own life when I have been asked to pray for someone in a tragic situation, and yet I have found myself thinking, *"Does my prayer even matter? Will it make any difference whatsoever in the final outcome?"* Such doubts leave me wracked with guilt.

And when I feel those doubts, I remember the story of Peter's miraculous escape from prison, and the prayer warriors who just couldn't believe that God would actually give them the very thing they had asked for. God knew exactly where these people were in their faith development. Did He punish them for failing to remember the miracle of chapter 5? Did He withhold His blessing and give them exactly what they feared was going to happen anyway? Not at all! In a move that would shock the early church, God rescued Peter from prison and certain death, and brought him safely back out into the world where he could continue to minister and share the glorious providence of God!

He did the same thing with a member of my church. A woman who was a close friend of our family and actively attending our congregation had tragically attempted to take her own life. Because of this, she ended up in a coma brought on by lack of oxygen to the brain. Consequently, she was severely brain-damaged and there wasn't any hope for her. Since she had no close family, she ended up becoming a ward of the state. My wife and I prayed intensely for her recovery. Others joined us in asking for God's mercy in her life. After many months, there had been no progress in her recovery whatsoever. Time continued to pass, and as years went by, we eventually lost touch with where she was and how she was doing. We firmly believed that she would be in a comatose state for the rest of her life.

Imagine my complete and total shock when one day, we received a phone call from a mutual friend, letting us know that she had come out of the coma. I couldn't even believe it. It had been five years. There was no way that she could come back after so much time had elapsed. In fact, the first words out of my mouth upon hearing that news were: *"That's impossible."* But God had been working within her all along, and He chose to do the miraculous. Though I would have never imagined that she would live a normal life after such a trauma, God had a different plan. Today, this woman is alive and well, and is married with two children. What an amazing miracle of God!

So whenever you start to think that your prayers are not important, or you find yourself doubting whether prayer can make any difference at all, remember Peter's story. When you are faced with a situation that appears hopeless, and you feel guilty for not believing that God can accomplish anything He chooses, reread this incredible account and reflect on the struggles of the early church. And the next time you run up against circumstances which seem impossible, remember that **"nothing is impossible with God"** (Luke 1:37)!

We pray: Lord, forgive us. In our hearts, we know that You can do anything. But many times, we doubt that You will hear and respond to our prayers. Thank You for Your Word that assures us that You remain in control even when our lives seem to be spinning out of control. We are thankful that Your actions in our lives are not dependent on how strongly we believe in them. Thank You for being the miraculous God that can accomplish anything! Increase our faith so that we will boldly ask for miracles, for all things are possible with

You in accordance with Your will. Remove any seeds of doubt in our hearts that would prevent us from crying out to You in prayer. In Jesus' name. Amen.

Athaliah: Nominated for the *Worst-Mother-of-the-Year* Award

When Athaliah the mother of Ahaziah saw that her son was dead, she proceeded to destroy the whole royal family. But Jehosheba, the daughter of King Jehoram and sister of Ahaziah, took Joash son of Ahaziah and stole him away from among the royal princes, who were about to be murdered. She put him and his nurse in a bedroom to hide him from Athaliah; so he was not killed. He remained hidden with his nurse at the temple of the LORD for six years while Athaliah ruled the land.

In the seventh year Jehoiada sent for the commanders of units of a hundred, the Carites and the guards and had them brought to him at the temple of the LORD. He made a covenant with them and put them under oath at the temple of the LORD. Then he showed them the king's son. He commanded them, saying, "This is what you are to do: You who are in the three companies that are going on duty on the Sabbath – a third of you guarding the royal palace, a third at the Sur Gate, and a third at the gate behind the guard, who take turns guarding the temple – and you who are in the other two companies that normally go off Sabbath duty are all to guard the temple for the king. Station yourselves around the king, each of you with weapon in hand. Anyone who approaches your ranks is to be put to death. Stay close to the king wherever he goes."

The commanders of units of a hundred did just as Jehoiada the priest ordered. Each one took his men – those who were going on duty on the Sabbath and those who were going off duty – and came to Jehoiada the priest. Then he gave the commanders the spears and shields that had belonged to King David and that were in the temple of the LORD. The guards, each with weapon in hand, stationed themselves around the king – near the altar and the temple, from the south side to the north side of the temple.

Jehoiada brought out the king's son and put the crown on him; he presented him with a copy of the covenant and proclaimed him king. They anointed him, and the people clapped their hands and shouted, "Long live the king!"

(2 Kings 11:1-12)

Have you ever felt as if God has abandoned you?

This question floods my mind with memories of the times I've felt precisely that way. Perhaps you, too, can recall events when you felt completely deserted by God to fend for yourself in a chaotic, cruel world.

And consider this follow-up question: How long did you feel that way?

As I reach into my own mental archives, there have been times when I felt that way for a relatively short time – say, a couple of days. But I can recall other times when I felt lost and alone for weeks on end, unable to feel God's presence or experience God's love.

When I have experienced such feelings of abandonment, I have found it difficult to hold onto the promises in the Bible. Sensitivities and emotions are so powerful, and can often distort the truth and deceive us into believing that there is something wrong with us. We wonder why our faith isn't as strong as it once was. In the chaotic mess of our lives, we attempt to hold onto God's Word, but often find it meaningless and irrelevant to our current situation. We try to override the emotions by reading and re-reading the promise Jesus gave us in the words spoken to His disciples in Matthew 28:20: **"And surely I am with you always, to the very end of the age."** Other people may try to comfort us with the assurance that He will **"never leave you nor forsake you,"** as promised in Deuteronomy 31:6,8 and re-quoted in Hebrews 13:5. But there are times when the hope it provides is not comforting, and we slip back into the feelings of despair. Perhaps we even start comparing ourselves to others around us who apparently have a durable and unshakable faith.

But even those with a robust faith will admit that there are times when they don't feel or perceive the presence of the Lord. Everyone experiences this struggle at one time or another, regardless of where we are in our walk with God. We all have moments when it may seem as if our prayers are getting lost in transit, and our cries are swallowed up by an empty sky. We still may be able to recall God's amazing promises, but given our painful circumstances, those promises feel hollow and unable to provide any real comfort.

We may cry out with the desperate words in Psalm 88:

> **Why, O LORD, do you reject me and hide your face from me? From my youth I have suffered and been close to death; I have borne your terrors and am in despair. Your wrath has swept over me; your terrors have destroyed me. All day long they surround me like a flood; they have completely**

engulfed me. You have taken from me friend and neighbor – darkness is my closest friend.

I believe we have all suffered in feeling abandoned by God. Maybe you are even experiencing that emotion right now.

The Israelites must have felt the same way in 2 Kings chapter 11. It was a dark time in the history of the Israelite nation. Due to civil unrest, the country had divided itself into two sections – the Northern Kingdom and the Southern Kingdom. Gone were the days of King Solomon and one united nation, ruled by those who follow after God. Quickly, the Northern Kingdom fell away from their love of God and started pursuing anything that tickled their fancy. As you go through First and Second Kings and the parallel material in First and Second Chronicles, you quickly discover that none of the kings who ruled in the north were followers of Yahweh. Instead, they pursued power and money, and ended up ruling with cruelty. The Southern Kingdom fared only slightly better as a handful of kings came and instituted reforms that aligned the nation back into the will of God. But those brighter moments of history were intertwined with times of savage ruling that caused even the most God-fearing man to begin to lose hope.

This was the case in 2 Kings chapter 8. An evil king had been on the throne for one full year. His name was Ahaziah and in verse 27 we read, **"He followed the ways of the house of Ahab and did evil in the eyes of the LORD."** Following his death and the end to his short reign, the unthinkable began to happen. Ahaziah's mother, Athaliah, decided that she wanted to rule the throne. Now, back in those times, if the king died, the monarchy would simply pass to the next closest relative. If someone was interested in seizing power, they needed to make sure that there were *no* survivors left in the royal lineage who could make a legitimate claim to the throne. Unfortunately for Athaliah, there were many relatives who were already in line for the throne ahead of her.

But this didn't deter her. 2 Kings 11:1 tells us: **"When Athaliah the mother of Ahaziah saw that her son was dead, she proceeded to destroy the whole royal family."**

I'm guessing she didn't receive many Mother's Day cards after that.

Determined to seize the throne for herself and assume supremacy in the land, Athaliah commits one of the greatest atrocities found in all of Scripture. She callously slaughters her own family, killing all of her children, grandchildren, nephews, and cousins. Pause for a moment and take that in. Instead of being a woman who loved and nurtured her family, she readily murdered those who trusted her and looked up to her. And it didn't matter how young they were – even infants and toddlers were coldly executed under her direction. Her remorseless heart felt no sympathy as she ran a sword through children and teenagers. It is incomprehensible to truly understand the absolute horror that her family went through as a result of her thirst for power.

And with that one quick move, it appeared as if Athaliah had destroyed a promise from God.

God had made a promise to David that a descendant of his would always remain on the throne (2 Chronicles 7:18). This promise was obviously very valuable to David and to those around him. An older David had once wanted to go out and do some additional giant-killing, but his men realized that it was not good to allow David to be put in harm's way. It finally got to the point where they had to tell David, **"Never**

again will you go out with us to battle, so that the lamp of Israel will not be extinguished" (2 Samuel 21:17). God continued to repeat His promise, even in the midst of evil and idolatry in the land with malevolent rulers in power, in 1 Kings 11:36, 1 Kings 15:4, and 2 Kings 8:19. This promise was tied up in the fact that there was a Messiah who was to come and rescue all mankind from sin, and that He was going to be a descendant of David. We can appreciate even more that if David's lamp was extinguished, so was the hope that a Savior was to come.

Yet because of Athaliah's heinous act, it now appeared as if all hope was lost and that the promise of God had been broken. This wicked woman secured her position in power by annihilating every remaining contender and declaring herself as the ruler in Judah. How tragic it must have been for all those living there who were devoted to the Torah and following the commands of God! They were forced to sit back and watch as evil reigned unfettered and unchallenged. I am sure they cried out day and night to God, and yet there was nothing happening in their reality that would give them any comfort whatsoever. How difficult it must have been to talk to their children about the hopelessness they felt. Their prayers to God must have seemed hollow and empty, for there was nothing in their lives that could provide even a shred of hope.

This is now beginning to sound like the despair and discouragement we often feel at the worst times in our lives. We look at our world and it doesn't appear as if God is interested in our circumstances or in the lives of the Christians around us. There is so much pain everywhere we turn. Satan is roaming around, wreaking havoc and leaving destruction in his path (cf. 1 Peter 5:8). As Steve Merkel put it in his song, "Lord Have Mercy" – *"Promises that burned within my heart have now grown dim."* And this feeling seems to grow more prevalent the longer it lingers in our life.

I am always so grateful to God when He lifts me up out of the slimy pit, sets my feet upon the solid rock, and secures my footing after I have been suffering in silence. I am especially grateful when I am lifted up soon after falling into (or being placed in) the pit. After all, I can handle the desperation and hopelessness for a couple of days. I might even be able to handle it for a week or two. Ask me to do it for a month, and I will admit that I don't think I am that strong. Tell me that I have to endure this situation for an entire year, and I would be horrified even to consider it.

Now imagine a scenario that is even worse. The Israelite nation felt abandoned by God. As far as they could see, the lamp had been extinguished from David's royal line, and the promise of God had been shattered. There was no hope to be found as long as the heartless Athaliah was ruling the land. And what's more, the painful despair caused by her reign didn't last for merely a couple of weeks or several months. Instead, it stretched for six excruciating years! Could you imagine being subjected to such evil for six long years? It's not hard to understand why the Israelites believed that God had abandoned His promise and His people. Was there any hope in this situation? Was God gone? Had evil won?

The answer is a resounding and emphatic NO!

God was working behind the scenes, crafting a suspenseful script with a surprise ending that would rival any Hollywood film today. You see, Ahaziah's sister, Jehosheba, had taken an incredible risk for the glory of God. At that time, she was married to the priest, Jehoiada (2 Chronicles 22:11). Jehosheba was gutsy enough to secretly grab Ahaziah's newborn son (her nephew) and stash him away inside the temple while Athaliah's killing spree was in full force – thereby saving one single remnant of the lineage of David. The eternal salvation of the world was now resting on the success of Jehosheba's actions to keep this child safe.

I admire Jehosheba for playing what must have been the greatest game of hide-and-seek ever. While Athaliah was running all over the place, trying to kill off all the heirs of Ahaziah, she astonishingly overlooked an infant who had just been born. And while Athaliah was busy rebuilding the temples of Baal around town, she apparently failed to peek inside the LORD's temple to see if anyone had been missed in the slaughter.

I would have loved to have been there in the temple, day after day, to watch the promise of God grow up! I wonder how often Jehoiada smiled over his wife's extreme act of courage. I'm also curious if any of the other priests ever wondered who this stinky rug rat was and why he was roaming loose inside God's temple, getting peanut butter-and-jelly hand-prints all over the walls. How often was worship interrupted by the squeals of a toddler? I wonder how the nurse managed to keep this kid quiet and out of the way.

Apparently, the news never reached the ears of Athaliah. Not once did she suspect that anything covert was happening right under her nose. It wouldn't have been hard for her to discover this child. Just one sacrifice at the temple or one simple visit to see what the priests were up to could have revealed this potential heir to the throne. But Athaliah wasn't the most religious of leaders. Her actions showed that she had no relationship with God. So there was no reason for her to step foot inside His temple. For six whole years, she smugly

reveled in her security, falsely believing that she had taken
care of any loose ends in destroying David's family.

This isn't the only time in Scripture when an infant was
rescued from certain death. Moses was saved as a baby from
the heinous law enacted at that time: **"Every Hebrew boy
that is born you must throw into the Nile"** (Exodus 1:22).
Moses' mom hid him for three months and then was able to
ensure his safety by getting him into the hands of Pharaoh's
daughter. To make sure the child was properly nursed,
Pharaoh's daughter ended up asking Moses' mother to take
over (Exodus 2:1-9). What a wonderfully ironic situation!
And think about the time when Joseph and Mary rescued
Jesus by fleeing to Egypt before King Herod killed every
male child recently born (Matthew 2:13-16). Both of these
scenarios are examples of people trying (unsuccessfully, I
might add) to thwart God's plan through their despicable
actions.

Eventually, the time finally came for the big reveal. In the
span of one afternoon, God clearly demonstrated that He had
never abandoned His people or His promise through those six
long years of oppression. What's more, Athaliah learned the
hard way that no matter how much evil is plotted in this
world, it will all come to ruin because of the love and mercy
of God.

Jehoiada makes preparations for the big event. The location is
to be the holy temple itself – the very place where God shows
His power and strength. Jehoiada informs the guards who are
coming on duty for the Sabbath day that they are to divide
into three companies and be stationed all around the area. He
even instructs those planning to take off for the Sabbath that
there would be some overtime work today. No one is to leave
for this momentous occasion. Their assignment is simple – to

protect the king at all costs. I wonder if anyone raised their hand at that point and asked, *"Umm...what king?"* For all they knew, Athaliah was in charge, and there was no one else remaining who would be able to rightfully claim the throne. Eventually, Jehoiada shows the guards exactly who is stepping up to wear the crown. Imagine their faces when he brings forward a seven-year-old kid! Not only were they going to crown the youngest king in history, but these guards were going to be part of one of the greatest overthrows in history, against one of the most evil women of history! They were all placed on "Secret Service" detail to make sure no one could come close to harming this boy-king.

Every detail is carefully prepared. Spears are handed out. Shields from the royal palace are gathered up and distributed. Everyone is stationed at their positions, and the stage is set. All during this time, people are gathering outside the temple and are most likely wondering why the palace guards are on high alert. And where is Athaliah while all this is going on? No one knows, but I can promise you that she wasn't given an invitation to this shindig. She had absolutely no idea that this momentous event was even happening. I picture her lying around back at the palace, eating bonbons and being mean.

Finally, Jehoiada presents the pint-sized king to the assembled throng. Instead of sitting in his room watching SpongeBob Squarepants[TM] like most other seven-year-olds, this boy is being proclaimed as the new king of Judah. The royal crown is placed on his head, the copy of the kingly covenant is placed in his hands, and he is anointed with oil. And then the people start shouting triumphantly, *"Long live the king! Long live the king!"* Finally, the long-awaited promise of God's love had been revealed. After six years of darkness and gloom, a light shines forth brightly for all to see.

The crowd goes wild and starts cheering. Trumpets are blown in jubilation. Kool & The Gang are there to lead everyone in a rockin' chorus of *"Celebrate Good Times (c'mon)!"* (Okay, I made that last part up.) Everyone is screaming and shouting, thanking God for hearing their cries and faithfully answering their prayers. A sense of relief must have washed over the people as these events started to sink in. They began to realize that Athaliah's reign of terror was finally over – and that God had been in control all this time! Spontaneous prayer would have been offered up as God's people gathered in groups in praise to their LORD. I have to wonder if anyone even stopped for a moment to ask, *"Where is Athaliah?"*

Looking up from her bonbons, Athaliah hears the sounds of joyful celebration, and suddenly realizes that something is not quite right. Why does everyone sound so *happy*? She races down the street toward the commotion at the temple, pushing her way through the crowds, ready to shout, *"Off with their heads!"* – when she catches sight of something completely shocking and unexpected. There, next to the temple column, in the spot where the king normally stands, is a seven-year-old boy with a royal crown adorning his little head, and guards protectively surrounding him. And guess what Athaliah shouts out:

"Treason! Treason!" (2 Kings 11:14).

Isn't that rich?

Here we have one of the most evil women in the history of the world – a heartless shrew who would readily kill you if you were related to her, a treacherous usurper of the throne of God – ironically whining, *"It's not fair!"*

It's okay if you break out in a little smile right here. We all delight in seeing justice finally prevail and watching as evil gets what it is due. I am sure that a snicker or two came from the crowd as this lady came storming forth, crying foul.

At this point, there is only one thing that can be done regarding the evil that had dominated the land – destroy it. So the soldiers drag Athaliah away from the temple and into the palace area in order to put her to death with the sword (2 Kings 11:20).

This story may have a familiar ring to it. The names and details are different, but what happened here actually happens again in Scripture. Thousands of years later, there was a man who came to this earth to be the one to fulfill the promise made to David that someone from his lineage would be the long-awaited Messiah. Jesus came to set up a kingdom that would never end. Sicknesses were healed, demons were cast out, and the dead were raised to life. People were overjoyed at the prospect that He was the one they've been waiting for all their lives. They would finally be set free! The crowds waved palm branches in honor of their king, crying out in joyful celebration.

But then the unthinkable happened. He was killed.

And it looked as though the promise had been broken. The people's hopes and dreams of freedom abruptly vanished as they watched Him be crucified and buried. It appeared that evil had won the day, and God was either uninterested or unable to stop these tragic events. The disciples scattered like frightened mice. The movement had been stopped. All the joy of the Palm Sunday parade quickly turned to complete and utter defeat. Many, I'm sure, felt foolish for having been duped into following this so-called Son of God who ended up dead. More were confused as they still held onto a belief that He was indeed the Messiah.

But that was not how the story ended. Once again, God was secretly writing an amazing script behind the scenes for the good of all mankind. In an unexpected plot twist that shocked hell itself – Jesus was alive! I have to wonder how the news got to Satan. I wonder what poor little devil was the first to come up to Lucifer and say, *"Um, excuse me, Prince of Darkness, sir? There's a slight problem."* And although Scripture doesn't record the fact, I wonder if Satan stormed on the scene and yelled, *"Hey! That's not fair!* Treason! Treason!*"* And there, standing in His usual spot, was Jesus, the King of the universe, very much alive and reigning on high.

We've seen this story play out many times in our own lives as well. During those times of despair, when it seems as if all hope is gone and there is nothing left to grab on to, Jesus is still reigning. Even after we've found ourselves clawing at the walls inside the slimy pits created by our own poor choices, God rescues us. He will *always* lift us out. Don't be discouraged if, in the midst of your pain, you can't seem to feel God beside you. Remember that feelings are transient; they will come and go. If we were to base our faith and our existence on how we are feeling at any particular moment, we would suffer miserably on a roller coaster of highs and lows. But for those of us who know Christ as our Savior, we cling tightly to something even more powerful than any emotion we can experience – the truth that He will always be with us. Feelings can change, but His presence remains constant. And although I wish I could assure you that you will be rescued from your painful afflictions and difficult circumstances today or tomorrow, it actually might be longer. It might be months. It could be a year. And in the case of the story of Athaliah, it might even be six years.

But I *can* promise you something else. When it finally does happen, you will be comforted and reassured by the fact that God never breaks His promises. You will rejoice in His unfailing love and provision for all of your needs.

And you will celebrate and shout, *"Long live the King!"*

We pray: Lord, there have been many times in my life when I have felt so lost and abandoned. I have even felt that all hope was lost, and that perhaps You had deserted me. In the darkest of times, I have been unable to see Your light and to trust in Your promises. Sometimes these periods of despair have lasted longer than I could have ever imagined, with no end in sight.

But I praise You, ever-reigning King, for You are always in control and ever mindful of all events in my life. Give me strength through the times in life when things don't make a whole lot of sense to me. When I feel that evil is dominating the landscape, remind me that no matter what is happening all around me, You are still seated firmly on the throne. Give me the courage to trust that when life is at its lowest and I feel that I am trapped helplessly in the pit, Your hand is near, ready to lift me out. And even when relief seems so far off, help me patiently to fix my eyes on Jesus, my Savior and Lord. Amen.

When You *Don't* Have a Lot on Your Plate

The apostles gathered around Jesus and reported to him all they had done and taught. Then, because so many people were coming and going that they did not even have a chance to eat, he said to them, "Come with me by yourselves to a quiet place and get some rest."

So they went away by themselves in a boat to a solitary place. But many who saw them leaving recognized them and ran on foot from all the towns and got there ahead of them. When Jesus landed and saw a large crowd, he had compassion on them, because they were like sheep without a shepherd. So he began teaching them many things.

By this time it was late in the day, so his disciples came to him. "This is a remote place," they said, "and it's already very late. Send the people away so that they can go to the surrounding countryside and villages and buy themselves something to eat."

But he answered, "You give them something to eat."

They said to him, "That would take more than half a year's wages! Are we to go and spend that much on bread and give it to them to eat?"

"How many loaves do you have?" he asked. "Go and see."

When they found out, they said, "Five – and two fish."

Then Jesus directed them to have all the people sit down in groups on the green grass. So they sat down in groups of hundreds and fifties. Taking the five loaves and the two fish and looking up to heaven, he gave thanks and broke the loaves. Then he gave them to his disciples to distribute to the people. He also divided the two fish among them all. They all ate and were satisfied, and the disciples picked up twelve basketfuls of broken pieces of bread and fish. The number of the men who had eaten was five thousand.

(Mark 6:30-44)

Do you ever wonder what life must have been like as one of Jesus' disciples? Sometimes, I imagine that things were pretty easy when Christ was physically present. I mean, the guy could do anything! If you needed some extra wine, He could provide it. If you were harassed by demons, Jesus had all the right words to say. If you were sinking or drowning, He would rescue you. And if you weren't sure which way to go, He would point you in the right direction. I envy the fact that the disciples had Jesus there with them in the flesh. There have certainly been times when I've wished Jesus could be here in physical form to provide advice or answers to my toughest problems, or to comfort me and alleviate my fears and doubts when life becomes uncertain.

But when I read a story like the Feeding of the 5,000, I step back and realize just how difficult it must have been to be a disciple of Jesus. He was always challenging them to grow spiritually, and to view things in a completely different light and from a heavenly perspective. How many times did Jesus ask them to step out in faith? Even when the disciples weren't responsible for performing the actual miracle, Jesus still actively involved them in carrying it out. Of course, they may not have always understood what was happening at the time. Perhaps there were moments when the disciples thought Jesus might be a little crazy when He asked them to do certain things that seemed illogical and impossible. And yet, as we consistently see in the Scriptures, they remained faithful in following through. This shows us that when it comes to our relationship with God, it's not necessary for us to fully understand everything before we follow where He leads us. It is simply enough to trust and obey.

In spite of any hesitations and doubts they might have had, I believe that the disciples showed more faith in this particular story in Scripture than many of us have shown in our entire lives.

An enormous crowd has gathered on the shore of the Sea of Galilee to hear Jesus teach. The word has gotten out that Jesus speaks words of truth with authority, and has the power to heal any disease. People from all over the area have traveled long distances to be in His presence. All four Gospel writers mention that there were about 5,000 men gathered in this one place. Matthew gives the added detail that this figure did not include the women and children. This little wrinkle makes it impossible for us to know just how many people were there, but it is safe to say that there are thousands of people present, all of whom are extremely hungry. This makes for a very unstable situation. I don't know about you, but I've been around hungry people before and it isn't a pretty sight. My wife knows just how grumpy and grouchy hungry men can become.

The details are a bit fuzzy on who spoke first. John records Jesus asking Philip, **"Where shall we buy bread for these people to eat?"** (John 6:5), while the other Gospel writers have the disciples approaching Jesus with this massive problem. Regardless of who first brought up the crisis, the disciples suggest that Jesus dismiss the crowd so that these hungry people could go into the surrounding villages to buy some food. But Jesus ignores this advice. Instead, Jesus sees a perfect opportunity to stretch the faith of the disciples. Rather than resolving the problem with His own power, He turns it over to His overwhelmed followers to remedy the situation.

"*You* give them something to eat," He tells them (Mark 6:37, emphasis added).[1]

Some quick calculations are made, and the disciples determine that even if they had as much as half a year's wages on hand, this amount still wouldn't be enough to provide sufficient food for so many people. If you want to contemporize this story, try this exercise. Take your own salary, figure out how much you would make in six months, and then ask yourself if you could take 5,000 men (plus women and children) out to eat. Would you have enough money? If we estimate that there were roughly 10,000 people there and it would cost about $10 per person to feed them properly in today's economy, then we are talking about a $100,000 food bill – and that doesn't include tax and tip! So you can imagine how helpless and desperate the disciples must have felt as they faced such an impossible scenario. John records that Andrew discovers a little kid with a lunch box filled with five small barley loaves and two small fish (John 6:9). But the disciples scoff at this proposal, knowing that a boy's meal wouldn't be enough to feed five guys, let alone 5,000!

We have all experienced situations where we've felt that what we have is simply not enough. At times, our resources seem insufficient to meet our needs (or the needs of others), and there don't seem to be adequate solutions for the problems we face. Maybe we don't have the "right" words to comfort our friend who has cancer. Or money is tight because we've been laid-off from work and our bank accounts are almost empty. Perhaps there just isn't enough time left to prepare for all those final exams or complete all the homework needed for school. And, like the disciples, we may stare at our meager resources with a sinking feeling in our hearts, knowing that it will never be enough. In fact, it may not even be close.

But it *is* enough for Jesus. He is willing and able to work with whatever we have to offer, even if it seems meager and completely insufficient. He always encourages us to come to Him with whatever scant resources we possess. You may feel that your words are inadequate to comfort your friend battling depression. Or perhaps you're worried that inexperience will prevent you from ever being an effective worker in God's kingdom. When these doubts and insecurities creep in, just remember this simple formula:

nothing + God = endless possibilities

So, in come the legendary five loaves of bread and two fish. Since we are guessing that this was some little boy's meal, it couldn't have amounted to much. Although my own sons have been known to consume vast amounts of food, even they couldn't finish off five full-sized loaves of Wonder® Bread. Rather, the loaves in the story appear to be fairly small – just enough to make a few sardine sandwiches. And what about these two fish? I highly doubt that they are twenty-pound tilapias fresh from the Sea of Galilee. After all, some child had to lug this stuff around. I imagine that we are talking about two smaller-sized sardines, which were common in those waters. All this would have added up to an adequate amount to feed a boy for lunch.

But was it enough for a famished crowd of 5,000-plus people?

Jesus takes the bread and the fish, gives thanks to God for them, and breaks them into pieces. He then distributes them to the disciples. In turn, the disciples take the food and begin to pass it out among the people.

Did you catch that? Did you notice the disciples courageously putting their faith into action? The story goes by rather quickly and it is easy to miss key details. It is in that very moment when one of the greatest demonstrations of belief takes place. The disciples took what Jesus gave them and actually started to hand it out to the crowd before them. That simple action required an enormous amount of confidence in Jesus and His instructions![2]

To better visualize the dire situation that the disciples faced, I encourage you to see it for yourself. Go into your kitchen and grab a plate. Then open a package of sliced sandwich bread, and take out enough to satisfy a young boy for lunch (perhaps two slices). Now take that bread and divide it into twelve portions – just as it was divided among the twelve disciples. I'm going to assume that you don't have a can of sardines hanging around in your cupboard, so grab some bologna out of the refrigerator. Take enough of that tasty mystery meat for a child's lunch – maybe one or two slices – and then divide the amount by 12. Set a chunk of bread and a piece of bologna together on a plate. Stare at that for a moment. This is roughly the amount of food that each disciple had to share with the multitudes. Not much, is it?

Now imagine you are outside with an enormous crowd of 5,000 hungry men plus a lot of hungry women and hungry children all staring at you with their big brown eyes. What would *you* do if Jesus handed you a plate with such a miniscule amount of food, and then told you to bring it to that first group of people sitting over there on the grass and offer it to them for their dinner? Be honest now. Would you have taken those steps of faith?

I admit that my faith would not have sprung into action right away. If I were in this story, I would have shuffled my feet, hemming and hawing for as long as possible. I might have voiced my opinion on the stupidity of this exercise, refusing to embarrass myself. There is no way I would have approached this enormous crowd with a few torn bits of bread and fish, risking the wrath of all those hungry people who were expecting to be fed.

But the disciples did it. Every Gospel text says that they took those courageous steps toward those groups of men, women, and children, and started handing out the food. I know that God was moving in their hearts, and the Holy Spirit was nudging their legs along to take each step in faith.

We don't know exactly when the miracle took place, but I can make an educated guess of when it did *not* happen. I highly doubt that the food increased in the hands of the disciples prior to them approaching the first group of people. For if Jesus multiplied the food before they even started their journey, their faith wouldn't have had the opportunity to grow. How hard would it be to hand out food to hungry people when I have more than enough already on my plate?

Now I admit that it would have been cool if Jesus would have snapped His fingers and instantaneously replaced the hunger within everyone's bellies with the sensation of being full and satisfied. And if I were Jesus (and aren't you glad I'm not), I would have raised my hands up to heaven, and legions of angels would have descended upon the crowd, bearing Whoppers® and fries for all! Even though heaven-sent burger combos would have satisfied their hunger – and probably made me quite popular among the multitude – it would have required no action from the disciples.

Many other miraculous events in the Bible share this common theme: God wants us to exercise our faith and step out in obedience before He makes His move. Consider the great miracle of Jesus turning water into wine (John 2:1-11). A great party is happening and people are celebrating at a wonderful marriage feast. But the wedding planner has failed, and the wine has completely run out. How fortunate they are that Jesus was in attendance – or at least, that's what His mother, Mary, believed! She goes to Jesus and informs Him that **"they have no more wine"** (verse 3). Hidden in this declaration is a request for Him to do something about it. Jesus, though initially put off by the appeal, eventually takes care of the wine shortage. Nearby were six stone jars that were used by the Jewish people for ceremonial washing. Jesus commands the servants to fill the jars with water, and then draw some out to take to the master of the banquet. I would love to have seen the look on the faces of the poor servants as they were given these instructions! *"You want me to do what? I'm supposed to give water to the master who's expecting wine?"* Incredibly, the servants obey this ridiculous-sounding directive. And with every step they take, nervously clutching that cup of water, they ponder a new career choice – for surely this will be their last day at work! But the story goes on to tell us that the master drank the water that had been turned into wine, and he was delighted with its superior quality. **"You have saved the best till now"** he exclaims (verse 10)!

I have to wonder – *when*, exactly, did that water turn into wine? Although no one knows for sure, the servants drew *water* (verse 9) and I suspect the transformation occurred only *after* the servants had brought it to the master. Now if the water had been turned into wine as soon as it was drawn from the jars, I'm sure it would be much easier for the servants to follow through with Jesus' request. But if the water remained as plain old water all the way until it reached the master's lips, then this simple act of obedience would serve to increase the faith of the servants in the one who made the initial request. The disciples, who were among the few people besides the servants privy to the miracle that had taken place, did just that and **"put their faith in him (Jesus)"** (verse 11, NIV 1984).

Or consider the crossing of the Jordan River. Joshua chapter 3 records this amazing event, which easily ranks up there with the other impressive water miracles in the Bible. The Israelite nation has finally made it to their final destination, the Promised Land! After feasting on manna and quail for some forty years, they can now just about taste the milk and honey that await them on the other side of the Jordan River. But there is just one problem – the river is at flood stage. With the depth of the water reaching up to twenty feet in some places, there appears to be no possibility of getting two million people across safely.

For three days, they camp at the banks of the flooded river, unsure of what to do next. Finally, God reveals to Joshua the action steps to be taken to get everyone across the river: **"Tell the priests who carry the ark of the covenant: 'When you reach the edge of the Jordan's waters, go and stand in the river'"** (verse 8). Joshua goes on to explain this somewhat unconventional plan to the Israelites (verses 9-13). I have to wonder how well this news was received by most of the assembled throng. You can almost hear the Israelites balking at this suggestion. *"Are you kidding me? This is the plan? The priests are just going to go stand out in that flooded river? Are you sure this is going to work?"* (Then again, this was not going to be the last time God had Joshua bring forth a ridiculous plan to the people; check out Joshua 6!) However, the officers embrace the plan in great faith and begin alerting the people that they will, in fact, be able to cross the turbulent waters after the priests have placed their feet in the river.

I am thankful that I was not one of the priests carrying the ark at that time. I'm sure that if I were one of the two guys up front, I would immediately switch places with one of the dudes in the back. I wouldn't be afraid to speak up and ask, *"Hey Frank... wasn't I in the front* last *week? Yeah, yeah, no more excuses. Get up here! It's* your *turn!"*

Whoever those two guys were that happened to be up front exhibited an incredibly strong faith. For Joshua instructs them that **"as soon as the priests who carry the ark of the LORD – the Lord of all the earth – set foot in the Jordan, its waters flowing downstream will be cut off and stand up in a heap"** (verse 13). Yes, you read that right. It was only *after* they set foot in the Jordan that the water would be cut off. Only *after* they had committed to certain death by drowning would God intervene and stop the flow of water.

I admit that I would be standing on that river bank for a very long time. I probably would have tried to strike a deal with God: *"Hey God, how about You stop the water first, and then I'll walk forward?"* Come to think of it, I would have even settled for the water to just slow down a bit! But if our faith and trust in God are to grow, then God will not stop the water first, or turn the water into wine first, or multiply the meager food first. He will want us to take the *step* first! Thankfully,

God knows how difficult it is to trust in some of His plans. It is at those times that He simply wants us to obey, even if we have trouble believing.

All this leads me to believe that even after Jesus gave the disciples their plates filled with small scraps of bread and fish, the food did not multiply immediately. Again, we don't know the actual mechanics of the miracle, but I envision that it was only *after* the disciples had reluctantly approached that first group of hungry people and offered the first tiny morsels that anything miraculous took place. That is a faith that trusts that Jesus' words and instructions can be believed. Sometimes, it is best to simply obey. That is why I am amazed at the disciples and their incredible faith. Every single one of them (including Judas!) went forth among the crowd with the hope that Jesus was going to accomplish something miraculous. That is the type of faith I would like to have.

How many of us are still standing with our small plate of food, or that cup of water, or hiding out in our tent that overlooks the Jordan River? How many times have we lamented that we haven't seen God do something miraculous for us, and yet our feet have remained frozen in fear and doubt? Is our ego still unshattered because we are unwilling to look stupid in the face of sure failure? Are we afraid to take that first ridiculous step, despite the promises that God has given us? As for myself, I fear that there have been times in my life when I've missed out on some powerful miracles simply because I lacked the courage to exercise my faith. ✝[4]

The disciples, on the other hand, were able to experience one of the greatest events ever recorded. They walked up to their respective groups and offered some food for the people to eat. I believe it is at this point when the miraculous event began to happen. After grabbing a small piece of bread and fish to give to the first person, they looked back at their plates and realized there's now more food there than there was before! Imagine the tremendous joy and relief that must have flooded their hearts as they realized that there would be *more* than enough food to satisfy the multitudes! God had indeed provided for the needs of His people, and in such a miraculous way. I know that if I were there, I would have shouted out, *"Food for everyone!"* Hunks of bread and fish would be flung far and wide for the people to eat. There would be no need to skimp on food, for it would be appearing faster than I could distribute it. Indeed, the food kept flowing from the plates of the disciples until everyone had plenty to eat.

As you can imagine, scholars and skeptics throughout the centuries have tried to discredit this miracle by offering up an alternative explanation. They claim that the people were so moved by the example of the boy sharing his meal that they all took whatever food they had and started sharing it with one another. What nonsense! If there had been that much food on hand, there would never have been a crisis in the first place. And even if everyone did share, there is no way they could have all eaten until they were completely full. Mark 6:42 states, **"They all ate and were satisfied."** Not one rumbling stomach remained! After the feeding frenzy, everyone loosened their belt just a bit and possibly even grabbed a food-induced nap.

The Gospels also reveal another important piece of the story. Twelve baskets were filled with the scraps collected after everyone had stuffed themselves. It is not hard to see that the twelve baskets of food were meant for the twelve waiters who distributed the food to the masses. As we can imagine, the disciples were so busy serving others that they never even thought to grab some dinner for themselves. I would have been tempted to grab a morsel or two, since I would've had no way of knowing if there would be anything left for me after this enormous crowd had dined. But these faithful men simply served, and now it was their turn to be fed and nourished. This demonstrates the reassuring truth that when we step out in faith and give to God what little we have for the benefit of others, we will not be left depleted. God will provide for our own needs as well. He will still feed us and nourish us – reminding us that *nothing + God = endless possibilities.* ✝[5]

This point was wonderfully illustrated in my congregation several years ago. There was a homeless gentleman, named Richard, who had started attending our Sunday morning services. Many of our members reached out to this man and cared for him in so many ways. One day, he suffered a massive stroke. Due to the swift action of the people in the church, we were able to get him medical attention rather quickly. But the damage was done and his speech capabilities were badly impaired. It became impossible to carry on a conversation with him; he could only speak pure jibberish. He needed intensive speech therapy to get him back to the point where he could communicate on the most basic of levels. But because he was homeless, with no money or insurance, obtaining solid medical care for him was challenging. Our congregation wanted to help him by raising funds to provide him with temporary housing and medical services. Our church was connected with a wonderful fraternal group, Thrivent Financial for Lutherans, which had a program that provided matching funds for people with extraordinary medical needs. Thrivent offered to provide $4,000 for Richard, if we were able to match that amount through our own donations.

What a great gift to be able to strive for! But I remember how helpless I felt. We were a small congregation of 50 people, and I wasn't sure if we could raise that much money. But we asked our members anyway, and left it up to them to decide how much to give. I could barely believe the overwhelming response of the people as we ended up collecting $5,000 for Richard in one Sunday! This means that, on average, every person gave $100. This is phenomenal giving that astounds me to this day.

And yet this is where I struggled in trusting that God would provide.

You would think that I was overjoyed at this incredible display of generosity. And don't get me wrong – part of me was extremely thankful that we had raised such a staggering sum of money. But mostly, my thoughts turned to selfishness. I started to worry that because the people donated so much money for Richard, there wouldn't be anything left for the general offering of the church. After all, we were a small group of people that often barely scraped by to cover the bills (as most churches do). A major decrease in giving might mean that I would go without a paycheck for that month. Would God provide for us? This is what was going through my mind at the time. But I was shocked and overwhelmed when the general church offering for that Sunday was counted and it was three times the amount that normally comes in! I could almost hear God saying to me, *"You of little faith! Do you think I would not provide for you if you stepped out in faith for me?"* How often I forget that God is in control! Instead of placing my complete trust in Him and allowing His spirit to guide me, I feel as if I have to take care of everything on my own. Yet in spite of my doubts, I am thankful that I obediently took that first step to provide for someone in need. Through this amazing demonstration of generosity in my congregation, God gave my faith an opportunity to grow.

I pray that you will come to realize that there are times in your life when God provides you with challenging experiences designed for your faith to develop. But to see it grow, you need to be willing to exercise that faith and trust that God will, in fact, come through. If your faith is not at that point yet, then God's invitation to you is simply to obey Him and trust that He will see you through. The temptation exists for us to stand idly by with our small plate of food. Will you resist God's instruction to share what is in your hands, or do you trust Him to multiply the food? Do you fear that the cup of water you offer to the master of the banquet will result in swift and certain punishment, or do you believe that God will turn water to wine? Are your toes remaining dry as you stand at the Jordan River, waiting for God to act first before you take that first foolish step, or do you have confidence that God will stop flowing rivers? Think about it this way: We have already placed our trust in God for the bigger blessing of eternal salvation. He alone saved us, and our lives have been turned over to Him for guidance. So what is stopping us from also surrendering the smaller concerns that we face each day?

What has God asked you to do lately? Have you been waiting for Him to make the first move so you don't end up looking like a fool? Perhaps today is the day that you stretch your faith and trust that God will come through for you. Do you trust that He will change the heart of your coworker if you share your faith with her? Do you believe that God will provide for your own needs if you step out in generosity toward the church? God wants you to have the confidence that you will, in fact, be changed by the power of the Holy Spirit when you step toward Him. Just remember all that God is able to do – even when you *don't* have a lot on your plate.

We pray: As we look at our lives, dear Lord, we shudder to think of how many miracles we have missed because we did not step out in faith. Forgive us, Lord, for not trusting in You or Your promise to provide for us. In our hands are but simple offerings to You. As we think of what we can give to the kingdom, we hang our heads in shame. Forgive us for becoming overwhelmed by our inadequacies and for despising the blessings in our lives. Instead, Lord, give us strength and courage to take whatever resources we have and use them for Your kingdom. May our stumbling, hesitant words accomplish all that You would want. May our small actions of kindness be multiplied by Your great power. May the time we devote to showing love to others be a gift that affects a multitude. And may our faith grow, Lord, as we step out to do great things that can only be accomplished through You. In the name of Jesus. Amen.

David & Goliath (for the Ultimate Fighting Championship)

David said to Saul, "Let no one lose heart on account of this Philistine; your servant will go and fight him."

Saul replied, "You are not able to go out against this Philistine and fight him; you are only a young man, and he has been a warrior from his youth."

But David said to Saul, "Your servant has been keeping his father's sheep. When a lion or a bear came and carried off a sheep from the flock, I went after it, struck it and rescued the sheep from its mouth. When it turned on me, I seized it by its hair, struck it and killed it. Your servant has killed both the lion and the bear; this uncircumcised Philistine will be like one of them, because he has defied the armies of the living God. The LORD who rescued me from the paw of the lion and the paw of the bear will rescue me from the hand of this Philistine."

Saul said to David, "Go, and the LORD be with you."

Then Saul dressed David in his own tunic. He put a coat of armor on him and a bronze helmet on his head. David fastened on his sword over the tunic and tried walking around, because he was not used to them.

"I cannot go in these," he said to Saul, "because I am not used to them." So he took them off. Then he took his staff in his hand, chose five smooth stones from the stream, put

them in the pouch of his shepherd's bag and, with his sling in his hand, approached the Philistine.

Meanwhile, the Philistine, with his shield bearer in front of him, kept coming closer to David. He looked David over and saw that he was little more than a boy, glowing with health and handsome, and he despised him. He said to David, "Am I a dog, that you come at me with sticks?" And the Philistine cursed David by his gods. "Come here," he said, "and I'll give your flesh to the birds and the wild animals!"

David said to the Philistine, "You come against me with sword and spear and javelin, but I come against you in the name of the LORD Almighty, the God of the armies of Israel, whom you have defied. This day the LORD will deliver you into my hands, and I'll strike you down and cut off your head. This very day I will give the carcasses of the Philistine army to the birds and the wild animals, and the whole world will know that there is a God in Israel. All those gathered here will know that it is not by sword or spear that the LORD saves; for the battle is the LORD's, and he will give all of you into our hands."

As the Philistine moved closer to attack him, David ran quickly toward the battle line to meet him. Reaching into his bag and taking out a stone, he slung it and struck the Philistine on the forehead. The stone sank into his forehead, and he fell facedown on the ground.

So David triumphed over the Philistine with a sling and a stone; without a sword in his hand he struck down the *Philistine and killed him.*

(1 Samuel 17:32-50)

Who doesn't love a good "underdog" story? We all love to root for the unlikely hero, the guy who has all the chips stacked against him. Something thrills us when we imagine the weakling standing up to the class bully or when the small town fights against the big corporation.

Maybe this is why the story of David and Goliath appeals to us so much. We've all pictured it – a tiny kid stands up against a monster of a man and succeeds in not only defying him but ultimately defeating him. It inspires us to think that as we face difficulties and challenges in life, there is no child of God too small and no enemy too great. This classic underdog story reminds us that we should never give up in the face of overwhelming circumstances. After all, if David could do it, we can too!

One of my favorite parts of the story is when David bravely marches out onto the field and confronts Goliath. The giant looks down and ridicules the competition standing in front of him. He even calls down a curse upon David (1 Samuel 17:43). An invitation to battle is issued, and David responds with inspiring words that we should etch in our hearts today.

> **You come against me with sword and spear and javelin, but I come against you in the name of the Lord Almighty, the God of the armies of Israel, whom you have defied** (1 Samuel 17:45). 2

Just reading this gives me goose bumps! David isn't afraid to stand up for the Lord. His tremendous bravery and his unwavering reliance upon God instill in us the courage to stand up to any problem we might face as well. Even when our difficulties might seem "Goliath" in nature, this story encourages us to trust that God will see us through. It gives us hope for those times in life when we appear to be out of options and we fear that we have no chance of survival in the direst of circumstances. It strengthens us when the doctors have determined that the cancer is too aggressive and there isn't anything that can be done. It comforts us when the money is simply not in the bank and we have no idea how we are going to make it through next month's bills. It soothes our worried souls when our resources have run dry, and we need to trust completely in the Lord.

✝ 3

But as we "Shake Scripture," there is another lesson God is communicating that broadens this story's application.

Close your eyes for a moment, and picture what this conflict might have looked like. How big is Goliath? How small is David? How hairy and scary is the giant? How weak and unimpressive is his competition? In our estimation, we usually imagine David as a pipsqueak with a high-pitched voice, and that the top of David's head barely reaches the bottom of Goliath's belt. Check out the illustrations in a Children's Bible or make a quick Google™ image search, and you'll soon discover that the vast majority of pictures are fairly similar. They normally portray Goliath as muscular with a six-pack for abs, while David is so slender that a breeze could knock him over. Goliath's scarred face is covered with a scraggly beard, while David's smooth, porcelain skin appears as delicate as the day he was born.

I'm not sure if that picture is entirely accurate.

Make no mistake about it – Goliath was huge! According to the measurements found in the text, he stood over nine feet tall and wore a helmet on his head that weighed 125 pounds. His neck alone was probably bigger than my thigh! The spear he carried was massive and held a 15-pound tip. Everything we imagine about Goliath's physical size and strength is probably correct. I'm sure it would only take a few battles inside the Octagon for him to be proclaimed the Heavyweight Champion of the World.

But let's consider David for a moment. It's easy for us to perceive him as small and weak. From the passages just prior to our story, we learn he is the youngest of eight brothers and is often left behind to tend the sheep. Although we may not know his exact age, we can estimate that he is somewhere between 14 and 20 years old. Yet, at this time in his life, he wasn't even allowed near the battlefield, but instead was relegated to the position of "errand boy," shuffling supplies back and forth among the "real men." But even though he was left out of the army, that doesn't mean David was weak in any sense of the word. I base this assessment on the description of David's hunting ability found in 1 Samuel 17:34-35:

> **David said to Saul, "Your servant has been keeping his father's sheep. When a lion or a bear came and carried off a sheep from the flock, I went after it, struck it and rescued the sheep from its mouth. When it turned on me, I seized it by its hair, struck it and killed it."**

This description of David's physical prowess is nothing short of amazing. He explains that while tending his sheep, if a lion (or tiger) or bear (oh my) came and snatched one of the sheep away, he would chase after the beast and engage it in hand-to-paw combat. If the animal was foolish enough to turn and attack, David would grab it with his bare hands and tear it to pieces.

I've been camping before and when we trekked into regions known to have bears, there was always a need to be extra cautious. Special containers called "bear bags" were a necessity. After a meal, all the food was diligently packed into these sacks and then suspended from a tree, raised high off the ground – out of reach of the tallest bear. Often we would change our clothes as well, since even the smallest of crumbs or faintest of smells from the day's meals would attract these hungry creatures.

But there were no bear bags for David. As a shepherd, he lived, ate, and slept next to the bear food. The sheep under his protection were an easy target for wild animals. Now, if I saw a bear lumbering toward my little lambs, I would gladly step aside and let him have one for a snack. I mean, it's only one sheep – there are plenty more. Besides, who's going to take care of the flock if I get eaten myself? But David was not that kind of shepherd. He would pursue any enemy and risk his life to protect those in his care.

In addition to David's extreme bravery in the face of wild animals, it is safe to say that he was much stronger than we normally give him credit for. Instead of relying on a shepherd's staff or other weapon to fight off the hungry beast that snatched his sheep, David would attack and kill it with his bare hands – HIS BARE HANDS! Consider the strength this guy must have had to be able to rip apart a wild animal with his bear, er, I mean, bare hands. I get the feeling that David would have had an excellent shot at being an Ultimate Fighting Champion.

It looks like it's time for us to update our mental picture of David again. Any guy who can kill wild beasts with his hands deserves to have some serious muscles painted onto his skinny frame!

Now what about David's size? We usually think of him as being small – maybe not even 5 feet tall – right? But why in the world do we make him out to be a shrimp? I'm guessing it's because of some assumptions we make based on the armor that Saul tries to give him in 1 Samuel 17:38-39:

> **Then Saul dressed David in his own tunic. He put a coat of armor on him and a bronze helmet on his head. David fastened on his sword over the tunic and tried walking around, because he was not used to them. "I cannot go in these," he said to Saul, "because I am not used to them." So he took them off.**

Did you catch that important detail? It says that when he put the armor and helmet on, he rejected the provisions *because he wasn't used to wearing them.* Notice that it doesn't describe the armor as being too big for him. He just doesn't like it because it wasn't familiar to him. Maybe he never wore armor before. It is the same uncomfortable feeling we would have if someone offered to loan us their stick shift car but we only know how to drive an automatic. Besides the common feeling of being uneasy using other people's things, we feel especially hesitant if it's something unfamiliar.

Now, it's possible that the armor and weapons *were* a tad too big. But that would be because Saul was one tall guy. Scripture's first description of him reads that he was **"an impressive young man without equal among the Israelites – a head taller than any of the others"** (1 Samuel 9:2, NIV 1984). So, because Saul is so tall, his armor wouldn't fit a normal person anyway. This gives us no indication that David is small. So go back to your mental picture and add a little height to this young man. There is no reason to think of him as eight years old, still wearing kid's clothing.

So why am I concerned about David's strength or stature? Do those details make any difference? While obviously the outcome is the same whether David was big or small, strong or weak, his physical abilities do affect how we can further apply this story to our lives.

If David is small and weak, then the lesson we learn is this: When we are ill-equipped or unable to survive against horrible circumstances, God is able to come in miraculously and do the impossible. When we have no other options available to us, then we must trust in His power. For some of us, it takes a complete absence of a "Plan B" before we learn to trust God in all circumstances.

But I don't think that is the case when it comes to David. You see, David had already experienced amazing victories fighting ferocious beasts. He held an impressive record and remained undefeated! By accomplishing those triumphs with his bare hands, he knew he didn't need to rely on any weapon, whether it be a sword or spear – or slingshot. According to the details we've discovered, David knew that he could contend with Goliath, regardless of whether he possessed weapons or armor. How could David be so confident? It's not from battling the lions and bears by himself. It's quite the contrary. David knew that it was God who provided this extraordinary physical adeptness, for he states: **"The LORD ... rescued me from the paw of the lion and the paw of the bear"** (1 Samuel 17:37). So, in his encounter with Goliath, David again relied on the strength God provides instead of his own physical prowess. And to make this clear to all, David chose an unimpressive weapon – a slingshot! With that unlikely choice, he was able to knock the giant down with a single stone in a shot that was truly one in a million. There is no way that David could take credit for such a lucky throw. Only God could have guided that tiny projectile past all of Goliath's armor and have it sink deep into his forehead. And by using a slingshot, obviously there's no way that David could take credit for overpowering and outmaneuvering Goliath by his own natural strength. By defeating Goliath the way he did, David demonstrates that he is fighting not with his fists, but with his faith. In the end, God gets all of the credit. And, of course, this is how it always should be.

Think of Gideon, the somewhat unheralded Old Testament hero. Judges 7 recounts the story of how this young man was used by God to defeat the mighty Midianite army. Israel had 32,000 men ready to enter into battle, but for the LORD, that was too many soldiers.

> **The LORD said to Gideon, "You have too many men. I cannot deliver Midian into their hands, or Israel would boast against me, 'My own strength has saved me.' Now announce to the army, 'Anyone who trembles with fear may turn back and leave Mount Gilead.'" So twenty-two thousand men left, while ten thousand remained. But the LORD said to Gideon, "There are still too many men. Take them down to the water, and I will thin them out for you there. If I say, 'This one shall go with you,' he shall go; but if I say, 'This one shall not go with you,' he shall not go." So Gideon took the men down to the water. There the LORD told him, "Separate those who lap the water with their tongues as a dog laps from those who kneel down to drink." Three hundred of them drank from cupped hands, lapping like dogs. All the rest got down on their knees to drink. The LORD said to Gideon, "With the three hundred men that lapped**

I will save you and give the Midianites into your hands. Let all the others go home" (Judges 7:2-7).

Can you imagine how ridiculous this must have seemed? God actually says there were *too many* men. He wants the army to be *smaller*. Why? He wants no one to claim that the power, strength, and size of the military were responsible for the victory! And just how many people were the Israelites supposed to fight on the battlefield that day? We read the description of the opposing army's forces in verse 12: **"The Midianites, the Amalekites and all the other eastern peoples had settled in the valley, thick as locusts. Their camels could no more be counted than the sand on the seashore."**

Oh my goodness! It would have been an absolute miracle if the original 32,000 men had been victorious in the first place! But to make sure that His people had no opportunity to boast in their own strength, God whittled that group down to 300. This ensured that all would know that God alone was responsible for the victory.

That is what I believe is happening with David. Instead of fighting with his bare hands, he fought with a sling. Instead of battling in his own power and strength, he used something that would allow God alone to receive credit for the victory. At the end of the battle, no one would be able to say that David did it on his own. Behind David was the LORD, who fought on his behalf. When we read the account of David and Goliath, we don't come away impressed with David and his abilities. Rather we come away in awe of how this giant was slayed by God!

How does this lesson apply to us today?

Often I believe I can tackle a problem all on my own. After all, I've proven many times that I have the skill, eloquence, or charisma to handle a variety of difficult situations. I've read enough leadership books to know how to respond in conflict situations. When asked to speak on a certain text, I am usually able to whip something up that pleases the audience. It then becomes a temptation to think that I can handle just about anything by my own natural ability – no God required.

Maybe you are a financial wizard and a monetary problem comes along. You've gone to school and have all the experience to solve any economic problem on your own. No need to consult God on this one. You've got it all figured out.

Maybe you're a talented musician serving in the Sunday morning worship band. Do you feel so comfortable in your own musical aptitude that there is no need for you to pray for God's help since you have had all the rehearsals necessary to get you through the worship set?

Or perhaps you are a surgeon about to remove the hundredth appendix that week. Is there a need to pray and ask God for steady hands and wise actions? You could practically perform this procedure in your sleep! Why ask God for any assistance?

I heard it often in my seminary preaching class: *Sometimes our greatest strength becomes our greatest weakness because we fail to rely on God.* You don't know how many times I've encountered talented people who could become amazing workers in the kingdom. Instead, they never realize their true potential because they have such raw, natural abilities. This proficiency lulls them into the false assurance that they can squeeze by without any Godly intervention or divine assistance. These people often miss seeing God work miracles in their lives, because they are happy to do everything on their own.

But consider that Jesus Himself followed the very important principle of only doing what His Father wanted. After healing a man, Jesus said, **"Very truly I tell you, the Son can do nothing by himself; he can do only what he sees his Father doing, because whatever the Father does the Son also does"** (John 5:19). Being God in the flesh, Jesus could have done anything He wanted while here on earth. But that isn't how Jesus did things. Instead, He was always seeking His Father's will.

How often have we been guilty of relying on our own strengths instead of relying on the one who bestowed them on us in the first place? When faced with a "giant" problem, instead of turning to the Lord, we often make the mistake of trusting in our own talents and power. The lesson we learn from David is that we should rely on God at all times and in all circumstances, even if we think we can handle it on our own.

So the next time a huge problem stares you down and taunts your God, don't begin to think how you should go about handling this one by yourself. Don't be tempted to live this life on your own. If you are confident that your strength will be sufficient, I urge you to seek God and see what He has to say about the situation. Put your ego aside, and allow Him to win the day and receive all the glory. This enables others to see the greatness of God. Let us proclaim with David: **"All those gathered here will know that it is not by sword or spear that the LORD saves; for the battle is the LORD's"!** (1 Samuel 17:47).

Join me in prayer: Dear Lord, forgive me. So many times in my life, I have tried to take care of the battles that come my way. Instead of turning to You and praying for Your wisdom and guidance, I often rush forth without giving You a second thought. I do thank You for all of the talents and abilities You have given me. Help me to live a life of thankfulness for these gifts. And the next time I encounter a challenge, whether it seems big or small, help me to turn to You first. May the strengths You give me be used by You in whatever way You see fit. Help me to trust in Your power and strength. And the next time a victory is proclaimed in my life, may I quickly turn it back to You in praise! For everything in my life, may You receive the glory, because of Jesus, my Lord. Amen.

Removing Rocks and Grave Clothes

Jesus, once more deeply moved, came to the tomb. It was a cave with a stone laid across the entrance. "Take away the stone," he said.

"But, Lord," said Martha, the sister of the dead man, "by this time there is a bad odor, for he has been there four days."

Then Jesus said, "Did I not tell you that if you believe, you will see the glory of God?"

So they took away the stone. Then Jesus looked up and said, "Father, I thank you that you have heard me. I knew that you always hear me, but I said this for the benefit of the people standing here, that they may believe that you sent me."

When he had said this, Jesus called in a loud voice, "Lazarus, come out!" The dead man came out, his hands and feet wrapped with strips of linen, and a cloth around his face.

Jesus said to them, "Take off the grave clothes and let him go."

Therefore many of the Jews who had come to visit Mary, and had seen what Jesus did, believed in him.

(John 11:38-45)

There's a familiar saying that goes something like this: *If you want something done right, you'd better do it yourself.* Seems like sound advice. Why rely on someone else to do the job, when it is often easier and faster to just take care of it on your own?

I can think of many times when I've found myself in this very situation. I've been in the middle of a home repair project that I simply *had* to finish, when one of my sons would come and ask to help. To be honest, I'd much rather just finish the project myself, since it would take much longer to complete it with my child's assistance. I remember other times when my wife was busy cooking something when another one of our sons would ask if he could help her finish preparing the meal. She would hesitate, imagining the mess it was going to make or the added time she would need to finish up. And just the other day, our youngest son was asked to do the vacuuming. In the amount of time it took me to explain how the vacuum works, what buttons to push to turn it on and off, and to instruct him on the importance of not ramming into every piece of furniture in its path, I could have finished the entire room myself. However, there's a reason why it's not always better for us to do everything ourselves. We know that it is important to include the people around us in our everyday lives. Our children love to interact with us and cherish being "daddy's (and mommy's) helper." The knowledge they receive and the skills they develop through the act of doing a task with us are so much greater than if they stood off to the side and merely watched us do it ourselves.

I have to wonder if God feels the same way about us! In comparison, we are clueless creatures who are constantly fouling things up. Despite our best intentions to serve Him and follow His instructions, we often make nothing more than a huge mess. We then end up begging God to come in and clean up after us. Wouldn't He be better off if He just did everything Himself? But time and time again throughout Scripture, God demonstrates that the best way for us to grow more deeply in our faith is not by sitting on the sidelines as a spectator, but by getting our hands dirty and participating in His work.

This is what makes this story of the raising of Lazarus so intriguing. You've got to admit that this is one incredible story. It is not every day that we see someone raised back to life! And along with the miracle come powerful words spoken by Jesus that continue to provide comfort to people to this very day. This is why I have, for so many years, over-looked some of the other details in the story that seem rather peculiar to me. I've never really taken the time to dig deeper in this passage of Scripture because it is hard to see past the fact that a dead man is now alive. But I can no longer gloss over these seemingly minor points because they have taught me a lesson about how God wants me to be a part of the story He writes in people's lives.

To better understand what I am referring to, let's go through John 11 a little more carefully. It is interesting to note that John is the only one of the Gospel writers to record the raising of Lazarus from the dead. In fact, he is the only one to mention Lazarus at all! (Luke records a story in chapter 16 that mentions a beggar named Lazarus, but the two are unrelated.)

At the beginning of chapter 11, we are introduced to a man named Lazarus and we learn right away that he is sick. In verse 5, we are also told that he is a man whom Jesus loved, along with his sisters Mary and Martha. Now apparently the illness that Lazarus is afflicted with is rather serious. In fact, the situation is so dire that Mary and Martha send word immediately to Jesus to inform Him that Lazarus, His dear friend, is near death. The sisters believe that if Jesus would come quickly, then Lazarus might be healed. Surprisingly, Jesus opts not to come right away – but rather He stays put for two extra days. He explains to His disciples that **"This sickness will not end in death"** (verse 4), and that He wants God's glory to be revealed and for the Son of Man to be glorified in the process. After the two days are up, He finally alerts His disciples that the time has come to pack up and head to Lazarus' house. He tells them plainly, **"Lazarus is dead"** (verse 14).

While Jesus is walking into town, a group of people have already gathered at the house to give their condolences to the grieving family. Somehow, the news is given that Jesus is close, so Martha rushes out to meet Him on the road. What follows is a touching encounter:

> **"Lord," Martha said to Jesus, "if you had been here, my brother would not have died. But I know that even now God will give you whatever you ask"** (John 11:21-22).

You can hear the grief in Martha's words as she comes awfully close to scolding Jesus for not coming sooner and saving her brother's life. But at the same time, this statement shows that Martha possesses a tremendous amount of faith – for she believes that if Jesus had come earlier, then Lazarus' death would have been prevented.

Jesus offers Martha comforting words by reassuring her that Lazarus will rise. Martha appears to be already aware of a future resurrection, for she responds, **"I know he will rise again in the resurrection at the last day"** (verse 24).

Jesus confirms her belief by uttering some of the greatest words spoken in the aftermath of the death of a loved one.

"I am the resurrection and the life. The one who believes in me will live, even though they die; and whoever lives by believing in me will never die" (John 11:25-26).

More beautiful words have never been spoken!

There is more to this story, although we don't usually hear the rest of it. From this point forward, pastors normally spend the rest of their sermon giving hope and comfort to those sitting in the church. At such times, the end of the account remains unexplored. I understand the temptation not to continue on in the text. Jesus speaks such a powerful statement of faith which provides light in the darkest of times. Hope is given to carry on in the face of enormous pain, especially when a loved one has died. There is comfort knowing that although they are gone, we will see them again. And this is a promise straight from Jesus. At that point, anything else might seem to pale in comparison to these amazing promises. But I would like us to take a closer look at the rest of this incredible story.

Remember that the discussion of Jesus being the resurrection and the life took place on the road into town. It was not heard by Mary and the others who had gathered at their house. After hearing Jesus speak these comforting words, Martha returns home and privately shares with her sister that Jesus has arrived and that He would like to speak with her. Mary heads out immediately to see Him. A group of the mourners from the house follow her, thinking that she is heading back to the tomb to grieve. But Mary is determined to see Jesus. When they finally meet, she falls at His feet, crying out in pain, **"Lord, if you had been here, my brother would not have**

died" (verse 32). This is almost exactly what Martha said to Him earlier. The two women have probably been discussing this disappointment with one another since their brother's death. It is interesting to note that no one is ever recorded to have died in the presence of Jesus. After seeing Jesus heal so many other people in His ministry, the sisters surely expect Him to do the same for Lazarus, especially since he was a dear friend.

The pain is too much for Mary to keep inside. Her emotions pour out as she weeps uncontrollably. Those who were following her are crying and wailing loudly as well. It seems that everyone is suffering from the pain of losing their beloved Lazarus. Then something surprising happens – Jesus gets upset.

Many translations of John 11:33 have Jesus becoming **"deeply moved in spirit and troubled."** However, I'm not convinced that the translation "deeply moved" accurately captures the emphasis that the Greek word actually conveys. The word being translated, ἐνεβριμήσατο (*enebrimesato*), is used only three other times in all of Scripture outside this story:

Matthew 9:30 – **Jesus** *warned them sternly*, **"See that no one knows about this."**

Mark 1:43 – **Jesus sent him away at once with a** *strong warning*

Mark 14:5 – **"It could have been sold for more than a year's wages and the money given to the poor."** **And they** *rebuked her harshly*.

From these examples, we can see that Jesus is not merely moved; it appears that He is angry and upset. What is interesting to note is that in the passages cited above, there is always someone toward whom the anger or harshness is directed. In Matthew's account, Jesus is speaking sternly to two blind men who received their sight. In Mark 1, Jesus is giving a strong warning to a man cleansed of leprosy. Mark 14 records the disciples harshly rebuking Mary who has just poured expensive oil on Jesus' head. (And it just so happens that the person they are rebuking is the same Mary from our story!) But in John 11, there is no person whom Jesus is angry with. He is simply mad at the situation.

I've felt that way before, and I'm sure you have too. All of us, at some time, have been touched by death – for it is an inevitable part of life. Sooner or later, someone we love will die. And one of the emotions we may feel in these situations is anger. ✝[2]

As I write this, I recently discovered that our neighbors down the street lost their five-month-old baby. The mother had just dropped off her older child at a baseball practice, and was heading back home. All during this time in the car, the baby was crying, suffering from colic. Suddenly, the sound of the crying changed drastically. The mother immediately stopped the car and pulled the baby out of the car seat. As she tried to console her baby, holding the infant close to her chest, the baby suddenly went limp and died.

I admit that I cannot possibly imagine the pain that this family, especially the mother, is going through. It is a tragedy that will stay with them for the rest of their lives. After hearing that story, I was mad. Of course, my anger wasn't directed toward any particular person. I was simply feeling deeply upset by this great tragedy – the death of a little child.

I suspect that this is how Jesus is feeling here in our text. Death remains an enemy for Him, and when He sees the pain and emotion that death causes, it's not hard to imagine Him upset and angry.

Jesus asks them where Lazarus is entombed. It might seem strange that Jesus suddenly needs to ask for directions. Certainly He already knew where Lazarus was buried. But Jesus makes this inquiry so that Mary, Martha, and all of the mourners will follow Him down to the tomb. And off they go to the gravesite.

Now remember that Lazarus has been dead for four days at this point, and the tomb had been sealed. The mourners all gather at the burial place. Jesus, seeing the pain that death has caused, cries as well. It is a tender moment where we see a more emotional side of Jesus. He doesn't pretend to have something in His eye or complain that the sun is too bright. He weeps, and is not afraid to have others take notice of it. By doing so, Jesus demonstrates that He is not a distanced, stoic person unable to show emotions. He also reveals another important thing – although He knows that Lazarus will be alive again soon, He is still greatly moved by the pain of those who mourn the loss of their loved one. This gives us the reassurance that Jesus truly cares about our own moments of suffering.

As they are all gathered outside the tomb, Jesus then orders them to do the unthinkable. **"Take away the stone,"** He says (verse 39). Doesn't this seem like a strange command to give in a graveyard? Can you imagine all the gasps and horrified expressions in the crowd? Martha is quick to protest: **"But, Lord … by this time there is a bad odor, for he has been there four days"** (verse 39). Or to put it more poetically, the King James Version states: But, Lord … **"he stinketh."**

Yes, I am sure that a dead body that had been lying in a tomb for four days would stinketh *a lot*! Especially in the Middle East and in the days before air conditioning, a body would have been well down the path of decomposition after four days. Given this amount of time in the heat, I sincerely doubt that Lazarus would have been recognizable by this point.

So considering the unpleasant sight and stench that undoubtedly awaited them inside the tomb, why does Jesus want the stone rolled away? In fact, if Jesus wanted to impress the crowd, why didn't He just move it Himself? If I were Jesus (and aren't you glad I'm not!), I would have levitated the rock in the air, Yoda-like, and thrown it across town, having it land on some Pharisee's house. Now that would have gotten everyone's attention! But instead, Jesus asks *the people* to roll the stone away. Why? Let's hold onto that question for a moment.

After a short prayer in which He gives thanks to God, Jesus exclaims, **"Lazarus, come out!"** (verse 43). And incredibly, out hobbles a man with strips of linen still wrapped around his hands and feet, and his face covered with a burial cloth. Sounds a little like a mummy, doesn't it? Seriously, that's what it would have looked like to you and me! Maybe Lazarus, freshly woken up from death, was even moaning and groaning. Oh, how I wish I could have seen this happen! I hope that when I get to heaven, God will show me what this looked like. From my vantage point, I can't help but smile as I play the scene in my head.

Can you picture the crowd's reaction as Lazarus staggers out of the tomb? I imagine that those present were completely shocked – and perhaps a little creeped out by the whole situation. Imagine that you are mourning the death of a brother or friend, when suddenly, you see someone (who you sure hope is Lazarus!) walking out of his tomb, wrapped up in burial clothes! Notice how nobody rushes up to Lazarus and gives him a big hug! Given the same circumstances, I don't think any of us would have the courage to approach someone who was freshly brought back from the grave, no matter how much we may have loved him! You also have to wonder what Lazarus was thinking this whole time. Did he even realize he had been dead? Or did he simply get up and walk out following Jesus' voice, wondering why all this cloth was wrapped over his face and limbs? I know I would be yelling: *"Get this stuff off me!"*

Finally, Jesus gives the instructions to free Lazarus from his deathly wraps. **"Jesus said to them, 'Take off the grave clothes and let him go'"** (verse 44). Again, I am sure there must have been some hesitancy to walk up to this guy who had been tomb-bound for four days, and assist him in removing his grave clothes! After all, no one had ever experienced anything quite like this before!

And yet I ask the question again: Why did Jesus instruct *those around him* to remove the grave clothes? Wouldn't it have been easier and far more dramatic for Jesus to levitate Lazarus, and then spin him around until the strips of cloth dropped like toilet paper to the ground? In my opinion, that would have been even more impressive. But surprisingly, Jesus wants the other people at the gravesite to remove rocks and grave clothes.

And He still wants us to do the same today.

These two extra details have helped me to understand that there is much more that Jesus wants to communicate to us regarding people who have been freshly "brought back from the dead." I believe that He is teaching us what it means to remove rocks and grave clothes for the people around us. These lessons may be easily applied to our dealings with those who are new to the Christian faith.

In the Bible, there are many analogies given that communicate the concept of coming to faith. One of the most popular is that of going from death into life:

> Romans 6:4 – **We were therefore buried with him through baptism into death in order that, just as Christ was raised from the dead through the glory of the Father, we too may live a new life.**

> Romans 8:10 – **But if Christ is in you, then even though your body is subject to death because of sin, the Spirit gives life because of righteousness.**

> Ephesians 2:4-5 – **But because of his great love for us, God, who is rich in mercy, made us alive with Christ even when we were dead in transgressions – it is by grace you have been saved.**

These are just a few of the passages that equate salvation with crossing over from death into life. With this in mind, let's take a closer look at the details related to the raising of Lazarus to learn some important lessons.

The first and most significant point is that there is no possible way that Lazarus could have made *himself* rise from the dead. There needed to be some outside power to bring him back to life. So make no mistake about it – God is the operating agent in salvation. It is He, and He alone, who is to receive the credit for bringing us (or anyone else) from death into life.

So what else is Jesus teaching us by having the people around Him remove the rock and the grave clothes? Let's start with the detail of the rock.

Many people are stuck in unbelief. They have massive hang-ups with certain aspects of the Christian faith. Imagine these doubts and concerns as huge boulders that are blocking their spiritual path. As God brings people into a saving faith and opens their hearts with His love, we should be ready to help open the doors to their "tombs" so that our brothers and sisters may stand freely among us as living, vibrant members of the faith community.

What are some spiritual obstacles that others may be struggling with? How can we help move these "boulders" out of the way?

Many people are confused or mistaken about what the Bible actually says. They may have heard only bits and pieces, and have drawn incorrect conclusions because they do not understand the true message. Others are quick to point to Scripture as a book filled with judgment, hypocrisy, contradictions, and outdated beliefs. I know people who have problems with the creation story in Genesis, because they've been taught (and possibly agree with) the theory of evolution. Many others struggle with the idea that there is only one way to heaven, preferring instead to believe that Christianity is only one of many paths to eternal life.

Some people were brought up in the Christian faith but have since walked away from the church, or even abandoned their beliefs. They may wrestle with memories of negative religious experiences from their past. Perhaps there was some emotional pain associated with attending church when they were younger. Maybe they were hurt spiritually by an unscrupulous pastor or from the politics within the church. Some may have felt rejected by self-righteous Christians who judged them harshly because of a mistake they made in their lives. Or perhaps they suffered a terrible tragedy and felt that God had let them down or even abandoned them. All of these individuals have some serious and challenging obstacles preventing them from becoming a part of the community of faith. ₃

Are you ready to help move some boulders? There are many ways we can make an important difference in someone's spiritual life. Do you feel comfortable discussing your faith with others, especially when someone has tough questions or wrestles with skepticism or doubt? We are told in 1 Peter 3:15 that we should **"Always be prepared to give an answer to everyone who asks you to give the reason for the hope that you have."** Are we willing to risk getting a little dirty moving some rocks, so that these people may not continue to push God away? Are we prepared to roll up our sleeves and help them overcome the pain of a past injustice or injury? Or do we simply not care, and say to ourselves, *"If God wants that rock to be moved, He will just have to do it Himself"*? Now, I agree that God doesn't really *need* us for the job; He is able to move whatever barriers might exist in a person's life. However, just as He asked the people standing around Lazarus' tomb to move the rock, He often asks us to help. But please don't make the mistake of thinking that you are the active agent in bringing people to salvation. God alone brings dead people back to life. However, we are given the awesome privilege of helping move the obstacles so that others may be brought fully into the Christian community. God actually wants us to be a part of the new life that people can have in Him! ₄

And what about these grave clothes? Again, I couldn't imagine what Lazarus must have smelled like and what foul stench lay in those grave clothes. And in a spiritual sense, when we are brought to new life in Christ, we may reek pretty badly ourselves! When we are new to the faith, we are just beginning to learn what it means to follow God and live as He would want us to live. The discipleship of new believers is a tremendous responsibility, and at times, it can prove to be a substantial challenge. When we come to faith, we don't instantly live a life of righteousness. In fact, far from it! New believers are often literally unaware of the commandments of God, and therefore have no real idea of how they are supposed to live. In other words, we stinketh!

I have known new Christians who continued to use profanity on a regular basis, or shack up with their girlfriends, or cheat on their taxes, or regularly participate in morally questionable activities. Oftentimes, I've heard lifelong Christians criticize these new believers for not immediately living a moral and righteous life. There seems to be a grand expectation for new Christians to suddenly have their life together and smelling like roses.

Just as those outside the tomb were instructed to unwrap the burial strips from Lazarus, God expects us to be active participants in "unbinding" our brothers and sisters who are new in the faith. He wants us to help them remove all those soiled, decaying layers of the past, so that they may be able to experience true freedom in Christ. Sometimes people resist and don't want to let go of what's familiar – even though it reeks and trips them up. They may be afraid to reveal to others what is underneath the top layers. Maybe there are addictions, sinful behaviors, and painful issues that will be brought to light and will need to be resolved. Often the unraveling process isn't easy or pleasant. But by involving us in this work, God is teaching us how important it is for us to be loving, patient, and merciful to others – just as He is with us.

What we are so quick to forget is that no matter how far we've grown in our faith, the smell of those old grave clothes still lingers on *all* of us while in this fallen world (cf. Romans 7:14-25). We will never be completely free from every remnant of the old self. And yet, instead of having empathy for others, we are often guilty of not wanting to help our neighbor remove their burial strips. In fact, sometimes we inadvertently bind them even tighter.

Unfortunately, I've seen a lot of insensitive behavior in churches when someone new comes in. Visitors are often unaware of the customs and traditions of the church, sticking out like sore thumbs to longtime church attendees. New folks sit in the "wrong" pew (heaven forbid that someone else takes our coveted seat!), their kids are noisy and talkative (because all children should know exactly how to behave in a church even if they have never stepped foot in one), and their shuffling of pages (in a fruitless effort to follow along with the service) creates a huge distraction for everyone around them. What do these new people receive in return for their courage to attend church for the first time? Often they get a lot of dirty looks and at least one person "shushing" them.

It happened to me, and I'm a pastor!

I'm not kidding. I was helping out in a special ceremony, but had mistakenly gone to the wrong church. By the time I finally arrived at the correct location, I was horribly late. I sat down near the back and started asking some of the people around me where we were in the service. I understand that being quiet is not one of my spiritual gifts, so even though I was doing my best to whisper, apparently it was too loud for some of the people in attendance. I actually had two ladies turn around and shush me! But instead of being annoyed or embarrassed by the situation, my heart began to break as I thought of all the other people who might find themselves in similar situations. What if I had been a visitor attending their church on a Sunday morning? I can easily imagine a confused newcomer asking for assistance from someone sitting nearby – only to be glared at and shushed! I don't know about you, but I would not consider that to be a very welcoming place. This might explain why many first-time visitors don't become second-time visitors.

This incident is a small example of a much larger issue. We are often impatient with new believers, expecting them to have their whole lives straightened out right from the start. We forget that they have just recently been saved. They are only beginning the process of living holy lives. And let's be honest here: Have any of us reached perfection? We all have areas in our own lives that still need a lot of work! Can we say we've figured everything out spiritually? Of course not! So instead of looking down on these folks, wouldn't it be better to rejoice in the fact that they have been saved? They have been rescued by God and have been given new life! And now they have made their way to church and have come to worship God. Wonderful! What's more, we have the privilege of lovingly sharing God's Word with them. By doing so, we help them remove the grave clothes and the stench associated with their former way of living.

[†]₅

Think of the people in your life. Do some of them have concerns and issues with the Christian faith? God might be asking you to roll up your sleeves and begin the laborious process of removing some of those rocks. Think about all the people in your own congregation. Do some of them stink?

Perhaps they need more love and grace in their lives, and fewer judgmental stares. Maybe God is calling you to help them remove some of their grave clothes. And for those of us who have kids whom we are trying to raise in a Christian home: Do we realize that they are still learning what it means to be a child of God? Do we have patience and love for them, knowing that God is still working in their lives?

And let us take a good look in the mirror. Do *we* still have some of the old grave clothes wrapped around us? As John writes, **"If we say we have no sin, we deceive ourselves and the truth is not in us"** (1 John 1:8). What vestiges of our old sinful self are we unable to shed? Where do we stinketh? Do we need others to help us to remove our own smelly clothes?

Now is the time to remove the rocks and the grave clothes.

We pray: Gracious Lord, thank You for Your amazing love that has called us from death into life. Thank You for the patient, understanding people You have placed in our lives to help us grow spiritually. In turn, give us the desire to help others. Bring to our attention those around us who are struggling because of some hindrance to faith. Give us the patience and determination to help remove those boulders from their lives. Make us mindful of those who may be struggling to live out the life You have planned for them. Give us the strength and courage to help them remove the grave clothes from their lives. And may our lives continue to reflect our gratitude for the life You gave for us – Jesus our Lord, in whose name we pray. Amen.

The Blind Spot

After he was weaned, she took the boy with her, young as he was, along with a three-year-old bull, an ephah of flour and a skin of wine, and brought him to the house of the LORD at Shiloh. When the bull had been sacrificed, they brought the boy to Eli, and she said to him, "Pardon me, my lord. As surely as you live, I am the woman who stood here beside you praying to the LORD. I prayed for this child, and the LORD has granted me what I asked of him. So now I give him to the LORD. For his whole life he will be given over to the LORD." And he worshiped the LORD there.

Eli's sons were scoundrels; they had no regard for the LORD.

This sin of the young men was very great in the LORD's sight, for they were treating the LORD's offering with contempt. But Samuel was ministering before the LORD – a boy wearing a linen ephod.

(1 Samuel 1:24-28, 2:12, and 2:17-18)

We all have it but we never like to talk about it – the blind spot.

This is a problem area in your life that you are unable to see clearly. It is a chronic sin or character flaw that you are not consciously aware of but is glaringly obvious to others.

Blind spots are different for each of us, and they manifest themselves in various ways. It is the woman who repeatedly marries the "wrong man," and can't seem to understand why she ends up divorced each time. Or maybe it's the father who treats his kids with harshness and cruelty, and yet doesn't understand why they don't want to be around him. It is the teenager who goes to parties and ends up drinking too much, and then wonders why he has no meaningful relationships and his life is in chaos.

We all have them, but we don't see them. That's why they are called blind spots.[1]

People in Scripture have them as well. Sampson couldn't see the obvious deception by his wife, Delilah (Judges 16). The Pharisees couldn't understand Jesus' rebukes of being unloving and unfaithful to God (Matthew 23). Jephthah was clueless as he made a rash vow to the LORD that cost him the life of his daughter (Judges 11).[2]

To help prove my point, I invite you to try this little experiment. Think of the people around you: family, friends, coworkers, classmates, fellow church members. Pick a few out. Now... can you tell me the mistakes they make in their lives? What are the sin issues they have? Perhaps your coworker is constantly gossiping about everyone in the office, which is affecting her chances for a promotion. Your neighbor swears frequently, and now his two young children have started picking up the profanity as well. Your friend shops too much and always overextends her credit cards, pushing her family into greater debt. Your brother becomes loud and abusive whenever he's had a few beers, and he is damaging his relationships with others. It is such an easy thing to see when standing back and staring at the lives of others.

Now start listing out the problems that *you* have. A little harder now, isn't it? We often have trouble recognizing our own flaws and sinful behavior, although our vision tends to be 20/20 when it comes to spotting the faults and errors of those around us. Jesus even points out this hypocrisy in Matthew 7:3 – **"Why do you look at the speck of sawdust in your brother's eye and pay no attention to the plank in your own eye?"** But I guarantee you this: If you are willing, you can easily discover many of the issues you have by asking others what they see in your life. I bet they have several things they would love to share with you about your behavior, lifestyle, or interpersonal skills, but they haven't done so for the sake of your relationship with them.

I see it every time *American Idol* begins a new season. Thousands of people audition with the hope of realizing their dreams to become a singer. Many of them have talent and skill vastly superior to my shower-singing. But there are always a few mixed in who just don't belong on stage. These are the ones with the blind spot. They have terrible voices that sound like cats falling from a twenty-story building (to paraphrase the former judge, Simon Cowell). But somehow, they have it stuck in their heads that they are the next greatest thing to come along since Mariah Carey. Often, their parents are standing right beside them, cheering them on – and they are equally oblivious to just how horrendous their son or daughter really sounds. They make tone-deaf statements like, *"My baby sings like an angel!"* Well, if that's what angels sound like, then we must not have ears in heaven!

In our text, we learn that Eli had a blind spot when it came to his kids as well. And this particular blind spot happens to be one that is common in today's world:

Eli honored his sons more than he honored the LORD.

This happens to be a blind spot that many parents are simply unable to see. Most of us who have kids firmly believe that we possess great parenting skills and everyone else should read a book on child-rearing. When this is what we believe, we are quick to point out how terrible other people are at raising their children, but we would *never* admit to having a blind spot in that area. That is Eli's problem.

I encourage you to go back and read 1 Samuel chapter 1. It is in this beginning material that we are introduced to the high priest, Eli. We also read of how a young boy named Samuel came to be under the authority and guardianship of Eli. It is a touching story of the LORD answering the prayers of Hannah (Samuel's mother) and Hannah offering back to God the very child she prayed for.

In chapter 2, we read Hannah's prayer of thanksgiving to the LORD. It reads much like the psalms that David offered to the LORD. It is beautiful in its majesty and honoring of the LORD for who He is and what He does. Her praise of God continues for ten verses which makes verse 12 such a difficult verse to read. It is jarring and upsetting compared to the material directly preceding it: **"Eli's sons were scoundrels; they had no regard for the LORD."** It is interesting to see the contrast in character between Eli's children and Hannah's child. Though all of them are being raised by the high priest, they have very different dispositions. This is most easily seen in verses 17 and 18:

> **This sin of the young men (Eli's children) was very great in the LORD's sight, for they were treating the LORD's offering with contempt. But Samuel was ministering before the LORD – a boy wearing a linen ephod.**

Here we have the high priest of all the land. He was the head honcho, religiously speaking, and his two sons were also priests. How strange that these two young men had all the opportunities to excel in life, and yet they end up causing so many problems for the people they are to be serving. Instead of using their status to encourage others to follow suit in godly living, their lives serve as stumbling blocks and end up causing great spiritual damage.

Now I must admit that there are times when parents do a fine job of raising their kids, yet when those children are older they choose to do things that truly wreck their lives and make a mockery out of the parents and their upbringing. Unfortunately, I have seen this happen to many parents, and there is very little they can do once kids are out from under their authority. But this is not the case with Eli. His two sons, Hophni and Phinehas, are still serving with their father who has authority over them. Eli has plenty of opportunities to make things right, and stand for truth. But as we delve further into the story, we see how large this blind spot really is.

> **Now it was the practice of the priests that, whenever any of the people offered a sacrifice, the priest's servant would come with a three-pronged fork in his hand while the meat was being boiled and would plunge the fork into the pan or kettle or caldron or pot. Whatever the fork brought up the priest would take for himself. This is how they treated all the Israelites who came to Shiloh. But even before the fat was burned, the priest's servant would come and say to the person who was sacrificing, "Give the priest some meat to roast; he won't accept boiled meat from you, but only raw." If the person said to him, "Let the fat be burned first, and then take whatever you want," the**

servant would answer, "No, hand it over now; if you don't, I'll take it by force." This sin of the young men was very great in the LORD's sight, for they were treating the LORD's offering with contempt (1 Samuel 2:13-17).

Here we read about one of two sins specifically mentioned in 1 Samuel regarding Hophni and Phinehas.

Now as you read those verses, it may not strike you as something that was inherently wrong. What is the big deal if instead of waiting for the offering to be boiled, Hophni and Phinehas demanded raw meat with the fat still on it? What we learn is that when someone was to make an offering of meat to the LORD, the fat was to be burned off and then the priests were allowed to take only a portion for themselves. This was how the priests and other workers of the LORD were able to survive in full-time ministry.

What happens here is that through spiritual strong-arming, Hophni and Phinehas took the parts that were specifically to be offered to God. Stealing from a man is one thing, but stealing from God is something that might prove to be more dangerous. And when it is combined with intimidation, this act becomes truly evil. No one likes a spiritual bully. All the while, there is the young boy, Samuel, watching and observing. He is growing up in the service of the LORD, but he can clearly see that his guardian doesn't even have the ability to confront and correct his biological children.

Over time, the blind spot changes a little. Instead of simply being oblivious to all the corruption that was going on under his nose, we learn that Eli had become aware of all the things that his sons were involved in. Now I don't know if there was ever a time that he tried to confront his wayward sons and subsequently failed, but we do know that instead of following the prescription that God has laid out for those who are sinning grievously and causing others to sin as well, Eli allowed them to continue to serve as priests. At the very least, he could have removed them from the priesthood, preventing them from causing further spiritual damage. According to Leviticus 22:9, **"The priests are to perform my service in such a way that they do not become guilty and die for treating it with contempt. I am the LORD, who makes them holy."** The priests were held to a much higher standard because of the spiritual influence they possessed. Their sinful behavior should have been corrected by Eli in some way. But that never took place. Add to it, we find out that Hophni and Phinehas engaged regularly in sexual promiscuity with women who also served at the tent of meeting. Eli's sons were sleeping around with ladies who had come to serve God. And sadly, Eli knew about it! Good grief! And to make matters worse, everyone else also knew about it! Eli was getting some of his information from people coming up to him and sharing the exploits of his children.

> **Now Eli, who was very old, heard about everything his sons were doing to all Israel and how they slept with the women who served at the entrance to the tent of meeting. So he said to them, "Why do you do such things? I hear from all the people about these wicked deeds of yours. No, my sons; the report I hear spreading among the LORD's people is not good. If one person sins against another, God may mediate for the offender; but if anyone sins against the LORD, who will intercede for them?"** (1 Samuel 2:22-25a).

Now, we have no reaction from Hophni and Phinehas. If I were a betting man, I would guess that they just laughed in their father's face. They had the perfect setup. They retained such power and control over people that they could essentially sin at will. There was no one who could do anything about it because their old man was too weak to call them out and require them to suffer the consequences of their sin. They were thoroughly entrenched in their sinful way of life, and were using their religious status as a cover-up for their sin.

Which then leads us to the last half of verse 25... a scary verse indeed.

His sons, however, did not listen to their father's rebuke, for it was the LORD's will to put them to death.

Whoa. This is about as harsh a statement as can be found in Scripture. Hopefully it doesn't cause anyone reading this to stumble. But we must come to understand that God does not delight in evil or wickedness. And there is even further condemnation for those who would use their spiritual authority to cause others to sin. This is the exact point that Jesus makes in Mark 9:42: **"If anyone causes one of these little ones – those who believe in me – to stumble, it would be better for them if a large millstone were hung around their neck and they were thrown into the sea."** God is so caring and protective of His people that if there be anyone out there who causes harm and offense that damages the faith of His children, He would rather see them taken out early before someone loses their faith in Him.

I think of all the damage that has been caused by pastors and church workers to people under their care. There are so many examples of pastors who have stolen money from the church, or staff members having affairs with each other. Youth workers have been removed from positions due to their struggle with pornography. To be sure, these sins can be forgiven, but all too often I don't hear repentant words coming from their mouths. Instead, flimsy excuses for their wretched behavior are offered up in order to save their own pride and ego from taking any damage. Even religious people caught in activities that are not God-pleasing are quick to shift the blame in order to save their own reputation. God has a serious problem with anyone who causes someone else to sin.

And then along comes a man of God. We don't know this man's name, only that he came with a message from the LORD to Eli. And this message was not going to be easy to give or receive.

> **Why do you scorn my sacrifice and offering that I prescribed for my dwelling? Why do you honor your sons more than me by fattening yourselves on the choice parts of every offering made by my people Israel?** (1 Samuel 2:29).

Ouch. Talk about having your blind spot revealed! Eli, though he was aware of the sins of his sons, had such a problem seeing the consequences of what he was doing by turning aside and not correcting the situation. This man of God says that Eli was honoring his sons more than he was honoring the LORD. Another interesting point is that the prophet of God asks Eli: **"Why do you honor your sons more than me by fattening *yourselves* (emphasis added) on the choice parts."** A case can be made that Eli was participating in the sins of his sons. It is plausible that he was uninterested in correcting his son's behaviors because he was benefitting as well. Eli is described as a heavy man in 1 Samuel 4:18. All too often, it isn't that we are completely unaware of our sins or the sins of our children, but rather it is a choice to remain the way we are and leave our family systems undisturbed because we benefit from it ourselves. Not only would Eli have to face the shame of his children being removed from their positions through banishment or death, but also he would lose out on fattening himself up.

This situation could no longer be ignored by God. To this day, God demonstrates His unfailing love for us by not standing idly by as we damage our lives by walking down a sinful path. The LORD graciously sent this prophet to give Eli the opportunity to repent and change. And the same thing happens for us today. How many times have you been caught in a blind spot, and people around you have lovingly pointed out your destructive behavior in the hope that positive change would come to your life? These people might actually be instruments of God's loving discipline, **"because the Lord disciplines the one he loves, and he chastens everyone he accepts as his son"** (Hebrews 12:6). Often, these people are our closest friends and advisors. And though the pain of their rebuke might last for a moment, their advice remains trustworthy. The writer of Proverbs 27:6 is astute in saying, **"Wounds from a friend can be trusted."**

Sometimes, our blind spots are things we are completely unable to see. Other times, our blind spots are caused by us consciously turning aside in the hope of not dealing with the problem at hand.

I know, I know. None of us would ever believe we have a blind spot like that. But it is called a blind spot for a reason. Eli failed to see that in his winking at sin, he was giving deference to, honor to, and putting more weight and importance to his kids rather than to the LORD. There are parents who have such a hard time correcting and speaking the truth in love, for they give more honor to their kids than to God. As mentioned earlier, some of the greatest blind spots that people can have are ones concerning their own children. People get extremely defensive about their parenting skills and shun the idea that their kids may not be perfect. Even humble, reasonable folks who can readily admit their shortcomings in other areas of their life tend to be very blind to their parenting mistakes! And yet this is an area where it can do the most damage because it affects the future of young lives. God is very clear in the Bible about discipline and training of children (cf. Proverbs 13:24, 19:18, 22:6, 23:13)! How often are children allowed to be disrespectful of their teachers, all the while problems with their study habits go uncorrected? I've witnessed kids destroy the reputations of their friends through gossip and malicious talk, only to have parents say, *"It's just a part of growing up."* Or when locker room hazing goes out of control, the parents quickly defend their teenager's sinful behavior by saying, *"Boys will be boys."*

A perfect example of this involved an incident with my oldest son, Mark Thomas. He is a very special child to our family, not because he is the oldest but because he is autistic. Several years ago, something happened to him that, to this day, still makes me shake my head in disbelief and anger. He was out at recess with all of the children in the school. Because he is autistic, he is often unaware of the world around him and the rules we live by. He was interested in sliding down the slide and simply bypassed all the children patiently waiting in line. Well, one kid became quite upset at what had happened. He pushed Mark Thomas to the ground and began kicking him. Thankfully, the adults on playground duty were quick to jump in and stop this kid from causing serious harm to my son. As they were stopping everything, they were asking what had happened. The other boy lied and said that my son had started it by pushing him first. My son has never picked a fight in his entire life. In fact, he is many times taken advantage of because he isn't interested in conflict.

The mother of the other boy was called in for a meeting to discuss her son's inappropriate behavior. Her response to the accusation was absolutely incredible. *"Well, my son didn't know that he's autistic."*

You have got to be kidding me! So it's okay for her son to beat up another kid who cuts in line, as long as he isn't autistic?

This lady was only interested in excusing her son's rotten behavior. It doesn't matter if my son is autistic or not. Her son's actions were inappropriate, and he should be disciplined as such. She is blind to her son's attitude, and she is blind to her own actions and how that could affect her child for the rest of his life. The lesson she taught him is that when things like this happen, blame others and justify your actions. Then you will never have to take ownership of your mistakes in life.[7]

God never intended us to walk this life alone (Genesis 2:18). He wants us to be a part of a community where we are open and honest enough to share our struggles, and loving enough to point out each other's blind spots. Unfortunately, society has been quite effective in convincing us that it is better just to mind our own business rather than become an interested party in the lives of other people. We are so worried about causing offense to someone else or damaging a close relationship that we tend to clam up and say nothing. It's like the wife who makes excuses for her husband's addiction, or the man who "looks the other way" when his friend cheats on his wife.

And it is easy to see why this problem becomes systemic. We become a part of the problem too because, let's face it, none of us like to have our faults pointed out to us! Think of the last time someone tried to share some correction in your life. How well did you receive that information? Were you quick to defend your actions? Did you scramble to think of something you could throw back in your friend's face? Maybe it is time to take a good hard look at ourselves. Do we simply live in denial of blind spots that have been pointed out to us several times? Instead, if we can take their observations with thankfulness and humility, our lives, and the lives of the people around us, can benefit greatly.

I also had a blind spot in my life, and it took all the courage I could muster to seek affirmation and help from my wife. I remember a time a few years ago when Heather and I were driving up to a wedding of a friend of ours. While in the car, I was thinking back to an incident I had recently experienced with our youngest son, Joshua. I had lost my temper and yelled at him, causing him to get visibly upset. The longer I thought about it, the more I realized that this had become something of a habit for me. I turned to Heather and asked her if I had been too hard on Joshua lately. She looked at me and said, *"Are you really interested in knowing the truth?"* Well, that answered my question! She shared with me that in her observation, I had become very critical of him and was quick to lose my patience. She shared that normally I am a patient man and can deal with a lot of difficult people and situations in life, but for some reason I wasn't giving that same concern to my son. Now that was some hard medicine to take. But I am glad I took it. I asked for her help in pointing out the times when I was "starting to lose it" with him. She agreed, and over the course of the next couple of weeks I was able to make some changes and correct my shortcomings.

So, are you ready for the challenge? I really am serious. The only way to see a blind spot is for someone else to point it out to you. Ask your spouse! Talk with your neighbor. Call up your sibling who knows you better than anyone. Find a friend you trust and ask them if they see something in your life that you aren't able to see. Be careful. No making excuses or justifying your actions. This is a time for you to listen to what others have to say, not jump in and defend yourself. Perhaps you've heard it before. Maybe you know areas where you are deficient but are unaware of the damage being caused. Simply sit and receive. And when they are done, thank them for their honesty in helping you out.

But don't stop there! It is one thing to have the blind spot revealed, but it is another thing entirely to take the necessary steps to correct your vision. Come up with an action plan that will help you make adjustments. Ask your friend to help you remain accountable. Invite your spouse to give daily encouragement to assist you in "seeing" more clearly. From there, take some time to make your confession to God. This is an important step in taking care of the sin in our lives. Share your heart with the Lord and speak to Him about your desire to change. Once that is done, you can have the complete assurance that your sins are forgiven. God delights in granting grace to His children when they seek His mercy. And then finally, pray for God's wisdom and strength to follow through in making the necessary changes in your life.

> **Search me, God, and know my heart; test me and know my anxious thoughts. See if there is any offensive way in me, and lead me in the way everlasting** (Psalm 139:23-24).

Dear Lord, we need Your help. There are things in our lives we cannot see. Search us and our lives, oh God, and reveal to us the things that need to be taken care of. Speak through our friends and family, and give us the peace to listen and accept. And when the blind spot is revealed, we ask for Your divine power to help us address the issues. Thank You for showing us our faults by Your Word, and still loving us despite them. And thank You for loving us enough not to leave us where we are. Move us by Your spirit and Your amazing grace. I once was lost, but now am found, was blind but now I see. Amen.

Shammah's Significance

Next to him was Shammah son of Agee the Hararite. When the Philistines banded together at a place where there was a field full of lentils, Israel's troops fled from them. But Shammah took his stand in the middle of the field. He defended it and struck the Philistines down, and the LORD brought about a great victory.

(2 Samuel 23:11-12)

Significance. We all yearn to be significant in life, in some way or another. Somewhere deep-seated in our psyche is the desire to have meaning and purpose in our existence beyond mere survival. Have you ever thought of *why* you are even alive? This is a question that we are often fearful of asking simply because we don't count ourselves as people who "matter." Sure, there are some who feel they have discovered their purpose, and have devoted their lives to fulfilling that purpose. But in my experience, most people don't think their existence is all that important.

Take a look at your life. What importance do you have? What significant events have happened? Do you look back with a small twinge of shame because you feel you haven't really accomplished anything? 🕈[1]

This world celebrates the "big." We love the superstars on the stage and the singers behind the microphones. We admire the speakers and leaders who make a difference in the world. The news cameras love the celebrities because they are larger than life. When we compare our lives to theirs, we may be tempted to view our own accomplishments as trivial or unimportant. Consequently, we may even wonder if anyone would miss us if we were gone.

The same is true inside the Christian world. Pastors compare themselves to one another based on the size of their congregation. Youth ministers are evaluated by the attendance they can bring in at fun events. We hear of "spectacular" evangelism campaigns where many souls are reached. So even in ministry circles, we measure ourselves against everyone else. *"Our church isn't growing as much as theirs. What's wrong with us?"* Maybe we minister to a couple of at-risk teenagers, but it pales in comparison to another church's ministry that has a 24-hour suicide hotline to help hundreds of kids every month. Our excitement can even turn to disappointment if we feel that we aren't making that big of a difference in this world.

Whenever these types of thoughts weigh you down, I want you to return to 2 Samuel 23 and reread the story of Shammah. I am drawn to this guy and what he did! In my opinion, he should be at the top of everyone's role model list. Although you may never have heard of him before, I am confident that you will come to admire him too. Shammah is counted as one of David's *Mighty Men*. I invite you turn back to verses 8-39 and acquaint yourself with the other members of this important group. These men formed an elite unit that David kept close to him for military maneuvers and for protection as a bodyguard detail. But Shammah wasn't just one of the Thirty (a cool title for the Mighty Men, even though there were more than thirty in the group). Shammah held a special place of honor as one of the Three, a trio of men who were extremely close to David, forming his inner circle. (This same arrangement is found in the life of one of David's descendants – Jesus. He selected twelve men among many followers which included an inner core of three men who were privy to much more.)

These three men must have been rather impressive warriors to be held in such high esteem by the man who killed a giant! In quick summary fashion, the writer of 2 Samuel lists the Three along with a story on each of them individually and collectively, highlighting their exceptional strength, valor, and honor (verses 8-17).

Clearly, Shammah was valued for his contributions. What was so special about him? Was he a charismatic leader? Did he rewrite the history books? Not really. In fact, I would characterize Shammah as an ordinary man who remains steadfast even when the task seems mundane – defending a lentil field (verses 11 and 12), and drawing water from a well (verses 15-17). In the former account, we read of a time when the Philistines (the sworn enemy of the Israelites) had taken over a lentil field. No further details are given on the importance of this field, its location, its owner, or its value. All we know is that the Philistines had banded together as a group in that field. Israel's army, for whatever reason, decided to hightail it out of there and live to fight another day. *All* of them scattered, except one – Shammah, who took his stand in the middle of the field.

The word that is translated as "took his stand" is a rather common word in the Hebrew language: יָצַב (*yasab*). Its most typical translation is simply "to stand." Some examples of this translation are:

> Zechariah 6:5 – **The angel answered me, "These are the four spirits of heaven, going out from *standing* in the presence of the Lord of the whole world."**

> 1 Samuel 3:10 – **The LORD came and *stood* there, calling as at the other times, "Samuel! Samuel!"**

> Psalm 5:5 – **The arrogant cannot *stand* in your presence. You hate all who do wrong.**

But many times, there is a deeper nuance that this word conveys. The person standing there is also standing *for* or *against* something. In other words, they are there for a distinct purpose.

An excellent example of the word being used in this manner is found in the book of Exodus, when God instructs Moses to go and confront Pharaoh.

> Exodus 8:20 – **Then the LORD said to Moses, "Get up early in the morning and *confront* Pharaoh as he goes to the river and say to him, 'This is what the LORD says: Let my people go, so that they may worship me.'"**

The command is essentially then repeated in Exodus 9:14. For me, there is something inspiring about this language. This word denotes the feeling of confrontation and conflict. In these particular instances, a barrier exists between the people of God and their freedom to worship Him. God instructs Moses to go and take a stand against that one person who would dare to get in the way.

The situation is very similar with Shammah. His story is about standing in confrontation against the Philistines. And he quickly discovered that when one attempts to stand against something, a conflict normally ensues. Shammah had to prepare himself for a battle and be willing to engage in conflict.

The Israelites were commanded to do this very thing in Exodus 14:13. They were caught between a rock and a hard place. In front of them was the massive Red Sea that blocked their escape route. And closing in quickly behind them was the enraged Egyptian army, intent on recapturing all of their slave labor that had recently been set free. As they stood there at that impossible place in life, **"Moses answered the people, 'Do not be afraid. *Stand firm* and you will see the deliverance the LORD will bring you today.'"**

Goliath also stood firm in preparation for battle as described in 1 Samuel 17:16. **"For forty days the Philistine came forward every morning and evening and took his *stand*."** Little did he know that he was soon going to be confronted by a young man who took his stand for God. And maybe that God-inspired bravery in that one-sided battle against Goliath was the impetus for David writing in Psalm 94:16, **"Who will rise up for me against the wicked? Who will take a *stand* for me against evildoers?"** [3]

I believe that the spirit of standing firm for the LORD is what drew David and Shammah together. Shammah was a man who wasn't afraid to stand in a field of lentils, even if it meant that he would stand alone.

I know what you might be thinking right now. You aren't really impressed with Shammah because he is defending a field of lentils. It doesn't seem like an important or momentous place to be willing to die for. What made this field so special? Is there something about lentils that we don't know about? Sure, it is one of the six ingredients listed in Ezekiel 4:9 that made up the bread that Ezekiel ate, and Esau did sell his birthright for a soup of lentils (Genesis 25:34). But this bushy plant is not a valuable commodity at all. Rather, it is a common food that can be grown in a variety of locations. Along with barley, it was a staple of the poor. So why not just surrender this plot of ground and find another field to cultivate? In the big scheme of life, who really cares?

Actually there is someone who cares a lot – the owner of the lentil field. For me, that is what makes this story so intriguing and Shammah so heroic. Sure, this farmer isn't even mentioned by name, and who knows what even took place after this? Was a memorial set up in honor of Shammah's triumphant stand or did the field just continue on producing a bunch of lentils? Whatever the case may be, Shammah was willing to defend a field that had all appearances of being insignificant. [4]

As Christians, we are often eager to do the big and grandiose things for God. We dream of the opportunity to be called to give a spectacular testimony of our faith in a way that has a huge impact in people's lives. We imagine standing in front of thousands of listeners and sharing the faith we have in Christ. We gravitate toward the stories of men and women who courageously stood against incredible odds and were ultimately hailed as victorious conquerors, like David against Goliath. The ministry of large congregations motivates us to grow from helping a few individuals to helping the masses. We long to make a powerful impact for God. We search for significance. [5]

Many miracles in the Bible highlight an individual who stepped out in tremendous faith and risked it all. Gideon faces an immeasurable enemy with only 300 soldiers (Judges 7). Moses trusted in the parting of the Red Sea (Exodus 14). Noah built a boat (Genesis 6). Along with these well-known stories are dozens of other examples of those who risked their lives to accomplish "big things." Some even sacrificed their lives on behalf of their faith. These are the kinds of powerful stories that we would all love to be a part of. We want to do something BIG!

The allure of those thoughts might lead us into a different kind of temptation. I think it is often in the smaller areas of life where we have trouble standing steadfast for the Lord. It is in the private moments when our faith may be put to the test. It is during those everyday interactions with our families, with the kids watching our every move, when we should be concerned. Think about how you live out your faith in the seemingly insignificant times. Imagine the life lessons we teach our children when we mistreat that waitress by belittling her for messing up our food order. Or when we have our children lie to their teachers that they were out sick, instead of telling the truth that we were at Disneyland. We might be tempted to dismiss those incidents as unimportant, but in fact, they aren't. It is in the day-to-day "lentil fields" where we face our greatest opportunities to take a stand for God and be a powerful witness to others.

We may tell ourselves that the smaller things don't matter in the grand scheme of life. Who cares if our kids see us contradicting our Christian values in the words we speak, or in the way we treat others? What is the big deal if, in the privacy of our own home, we fail to honor God through our thoughts and actions? In our mind, we often minimize the impact we have in the areas of life that touch only one or two people. We also have a tendency to discount the value of something positive we do, if no one is there to see it. For example, we are often tempted to engage only in activities that are visible to many others. We can fall into the trap of thinking nothing can be significant unless it is recognized.

We might think Shammah is ridiculous for standing alone against the enemy in a lentil field, because we can't comprehend its significance. But imagine the owner of that field and the gratitude he must have felt. Think of the witness Shammah gave as he refused to back down in the face of the enemy, even in an "insignificant" place.

Frankly, we need more people like Shammah. Or better yet, WE need to be people like Shammah!

It reminds me of an old, but cute little tale. A man was walking along the beach, picking up starfish that had been washed ashore. If left in the sun, these helpless creatures would simply bake to death. This man would bend over and pick up one starfish after another, and fling them back to safety in the ocean. A casual observer came by and tried to reason with the man. *"There are so many starfish dying here on the beach that it is impossible for you to save them all. Do you think you are making some sort of difference in the starfish world by grabbing a tiny percentage of them and tossing them back in the water?"*

The man stood there with a starfish in his hand. Throwing it out far into the water, he said, *"I just made a difference for that one!"* (from *The Star Thrower* by Loren Eiseley; Times Books, 1978; pp. 169-186).

Is there a lentil field nearby that needs defending? Is there someone who needs you to come and take a stand beside them? Is there something small that can be done for the sake of God and others?

I understand how difficult it is for us to feel significant in a world where big things are happening around us every day. When I hear of churches that minister to thousands of homeless people every week, it makes me wonder how important it is that our congregation is reaching only about 25 such people. In the grand scheme of things, it appears rather unimpressive. I read of doctors and nurses in third world countries performing life saving actions, which makes me doubt the importance of my donating a few pints of blood. When I think of people devoting their lives to kids with special needs, I examine my life and quickly dismiss my own good work as shallow in comparison.

We often despise the little things we do in life. A danger of believing our actions are unimportant is that we might end up doing nothing at all. Shammah might have faced that same temptation as he looked over that lentil field. Is it possible that he entertained the thought: *"What kind of difference am I really making here? Who really cares?"*

Consider God's word in Zechariah 4:10 – **"Who despises the day of small things? Men will rejoice when they see the plumb line in the hand of Zerubbabel"** (NIV 1984). Who is this Zerubbabel character and what is this reference to the day of small things?

The Israelite people had been taken into captivity after decades of disobedience. For seventy years, they had suffered in a foreign land under foreign oppression. Finally, they were set free to return to their homeland and rebuild their lives. A large group under the leadership of a man named Zerubbabel returned and immediately organized the rebuilding of the temple. After succeeding in the "small thing" of laying the foundation, an impromptu worship service broke out. People were dancing and singing and praising God. But not everyone was joining in the celebration. Among those who had returned were a group of people who compared this tiny accomplishment to the temple from their glory days. They started weeping and wailing in the midst of the party. It got so bad that: **"No one could distinguish the sound of the shouts**

of joy from the sound of weeping, because the people made so much noise. And the sound was heard far away" (Ezra 3:13).

Instead of focusing on the joy that was theirs because the temple was being rebuilt after lying in ruins, many were playing the comparison game. Rather than rejoicing in the "day of small things" that was before them, they lamented that it wasn't as good as it was in the past. And how often have we been guilty of using other people's accomplishments as a measuring stick against our own?

Jesus didn't despise the little things in life. Have you noticed how often we find Him ministering to only one person? For example, in John chapter 5, Jesus is in Jerusalem at a pool where disabled people came to find healing. Some manuscripts inform us that there was a superstition among the group that every so often, an angel of the Lord would come and stir the waters. The lucky person who was the first to get into the pool after the water was disturbed would be cured of whatever disease they had. Not surprisingly, this pool was surrounded by dozens of invalids and sick people, all hoping to be healed.

Jesus approaches one of the men and asks him if he desires to be healed. The man confesses that he has no one to help him into the water. He laments that every time the water bubbles, someone else jumps in before him. This man had been an invalid for 38 years and must have spent many of those years at the edge of the water, hoping for a miracle. After all that waiting, Jesus comes along and simply proclaims him healed. After being unable to walk for 38 years, the gentleman stands up, grabs his mat, and starts walking.

There are so many lessons to learn from this one little story. But what I want you to notice now is that there is no mention of anyone else being healed by Jesus that day by the pool. That one man alone receives the benefit of Jesus' miraculous healing power. I've often wondered, *"How come Jesus didn't heal everyone else sitting there? Why only that one person?"* I could spend my whole life speculating on Jesus' motives, but what I do know is that Jesus will go to great lengths and do miraculous things for just one person.

Some might think, *"What a waste! There are so many others in need. There is so much more to be done."* This is what we often think when faced with a world filled with tragedy, pain, and difficulties. What difference can *we* possibly make? For Jesus, it was enough to make a difference in that one man's life that day. † ₆

This is what Jesus is communicating to us when He shares, **"I tell you the truth, anyone who gives you a cup of water in my name because you belong to Christ will certainly not lose his reward"** (Mark 9:41, NIV 1984). If you do something as simple as offering a little child a cup of water in Jesus' name, He sees your good deed and blesses you for it.

And this is exactly what Shammah was doing! He was defending a lentil field in the name of God. And while it might seem insignificant and unimportant, it is given to us as an example of how all of us should be actively pursuing the small things of God.

Maybe there is a preschool class that needs a volunteer to bake cookies. Sure, you won't receive nationwide coverage for combining sugar, flour, and eggs for a few high-strung toddlers. But think of the message that you are sending to those little children – they are special enough for someone to come and do something nice for them.

Maybe there is a prison ministry, and you decide to participate by simply speaking kind and tender-hearted words. I agree, the nightly news won't show up in awe of your willingness to be among convicts. But think of the message you will be sending to those people – they are special and valuable to God.

Maybe there is a spouse that needs you to be more available around the house. You aren't going to be receiving the Nobel Peace Prize, but imagine what a loving example you give to your spouse, children, and neighbors.

I would dare say that more good can be done by 100 Shammahs taking their stand in a lentil field than one man slaying a giant. The impact of Christians taking a stand for all the right things in all the small ways could actually transform their families, communities, and world!

What do you need to take a stand for? Where is your lentil field? What one small thing can you do today to honor God?

Whatever you do, you can be assured of one thing that will come from your small stand – God will bring about a great victory (cf. 2 Samuel 23:12).

We pray: Lord, I have often wished to do great things for You, but not for Your glory – rather because of my own selfish pride. Day after day, I miss the opportunities You place before me to do the little things. Open my eyes to see all the great things to be accomplished today. Help me to love my spouse, speak kind words to my neighbor, and show grace to those who need it the most. Give me the strength of

Shammah to defend the lentil fields around me. Grant me boldness to stand for You in every aspect of my life. Thank You for Your care and concern over all the little things in my life. And may I stand strong in Your power! I pray this all in Jesus' name. Amen.

162

Careful, That First Step Is a Doozy!

Immediately Jesus made the disciples get into the boat and go on ahead of him to the other side, while he dismissed the crowd. After he had dismissed them, he went up on a mountainside by himself to pray. Later that night, he was there alone, and the boat was already a considerable distance from land, buffeted by the waves because the wind was against it.

Shortly before dawn Jesus went out to them, walking on the lake. When the disciples saw him walking on the lake, they were terrified. "It's a ghost," they said, and cried out in fear.

But Jesus immediately said to them: "Take courage! It is I. Don't be afraid."

"Lord, if it's you," Peter replied, "tell me to come to you on the water."

"Come," he said.

Then Peter got down out of the boat, walked on the water and came toward Jesus. But when he saw the wind, he was afraid and, beginning to sink, cried out, "Lord, save me!"

Immediately Jesus reached out his hand and caught him. "You of little faith," he said, "why did you doubt?"

And when they climbed into the boat, the wind died down.
Then those who were in the boat worshiped him, saying,
"Truly you are the Son of God."

(Matthew 14:22-33)

Have you ever actually tried walking on water? As a kid, I
was fascinated by Jesus' ability to walk across the top of the
waves and His power to allow others to do the same. There
have been times when I've prayed before putting my foot on
the surface of the water, hoping that it would miraculously be
able to hold my weight. Sadly, it never worked! I admit that I
have never had the guts to try this while fully dressed in my
street clothes. Instead, each attempt was made while I was
already bare-footed and dressed in my swim trunks. And
there would be no way that I would have ever announced my
intentions to anyone around me, because I always had the
"sinking" feeling that it would never work.

Even those who wouldn't call themselves "Christian" have
heard about Jesus and Peter walking on the water. There is
even a type of lizard, called a basilisk, that has the ability to
run on the surface of the water. This unusual trait has earned
him the affectionate nickname of the "Jesus Christ Lizard."
Several videos on YouTube[TM] show this animal with its
incredible ability to walk on water.

As you read the Biblical account above of Peter and Jesus
walking on the water, does a mental image form in your mind
of what might have taken place that night? If you've been a
church-going Christian for any amount of time, then chances
are good that you've heard this story explained in a sermon. It
is also a favorite lesson taught in Sunday school classes
because of the fascination it evokes in children. Most of us

have been exposed to at least one painting or flannelgraph of this incredible event. But if this is your first time ever reading this story, then you are in for a treat.

Most sermons on this passage emphasize the Lordship of Jesus and His power over the natural elements – and well they should. He is God over all; He can command anything from His creation, and it will obey Him. The second most commonly preached aspect of this passage focuses on Peter's initial bravery in walking on water, followed by his lack of faith as he falls below the surface of the water. Pastors love to talk about Peter's failure here. The point is made that if Peter had kept his eyes focused on Jesus, he would have never started to sink. The natural application here is that although we suffer in the "storms of life," as long as our gaze remains on the Lord, we too can overcome great difficulty and "rise above" the chaos.

Yeah… I don't think so.

The application sounds reasonable enough, but it reveals our lack of understanding of all the details provided in the Gospels. I believe it is our faulty mental image of this story that causes the most confusion in our understanding. Add in the dozens of historical paintings of this scene, and it's no wonder we have an incomplete and distorted view of Jesus, Peter, and ourselves.

Take a look on the Internet. Type "Jesus walks on water paintings" into any search engine and you can browse through several different renderings of this account. All of the images that I discovered failed to accurately reflect many of the crucial details provided for us in Scripture. This incorrect information distorts the truth and its application.

You've already read Matthew's account of the story provided at the beginning of this devotion. I also invite you to check out the other two times it is recounted in Scripture (Mark 6:45-51 and John 6:15-21). This will help you to familiarize yourself with the finer points of this story, as different writers record different details about this incredible event. As we put it all together, a more complete picture of the event emerges.

Let's dig deeper into what the text actually says, and then zoom out to grasp the overall picture. Once this is done, we will be able to appreciate the richness of this story and how it *really* applies to us. So now I invite you to clear your mind. Blacken the canvas. As you read along, take careful note of specific details. Paint a vivid and realistic picture.

What a glorious day it had been for the disciples! They had been witnesses and participants in the seemingly impossible feeding of thousands of people (Matthew 14:13-21). I can imagine them basking in the afterglow of this amazing miracle. But their Lord doesn't allow them time for pats on the back. Immediately, He instructs them to board their boat and start sailing ahead of Him on the lake.

"Point the boat toward Bethsaida" (cf. Mark 6:45), Jesus says, and off they go. But Jesus doesn't join them. Instead, He heads up the mountainside for an all-night conversation with His Dad. During this time, we read that a **"strong wind was blowing"** (John 6:18). This did not hamper Jesus' prayer time in the slightest. It didn't matter how hard the wind was blowing. Although we probably can't imagine choosing to pray outside during a wind storm, Jesus couldn't imagine being anywhere else.

Meanwhile, back at the boat, trouble begins. These seasoned fishermen were about to experience what must have been one of the worst storms of their lives. According to Mark, they are stuck in the middle of the Sea of Galilee (6:47-48). And since this lake is seven miles wide, they are smack-dab in the center of a potentially deadly situation.

John says that the water was rough and that the wind was strong (6:18). Matthew states, **"but the boat was already a considerable distance from land, buffeted by the waves because the wind was against it"** (14:24).

Waves "buffeted" the boat? Now, I admit that I had no idea what that word meant. It's not a regular part of my vocabulary. So I did what my 3rd grade teacher told me to do – I looked it up. I discovered that buffeted means to knock someone or something about; to batter repeatedly. (Why the translators chose such an obscure word as "buffeted" I will never know. Sure, the definition is spot-on, but who uses words like that?) To help us understand this word further and how it is used in other parts of Scripture, let's go back to the original Greek. The word here is βασανιζόμενον *(basanizomenon)*. Matthew uses this same word two other times in his Gospel, and in both cases something other than "buffeted" is used in translation. In Matthew 8:6, we read of a centurion who has come to ask Jesus for help. **"Lord,"** he says, **"my servant lies at home paralyzed, suffering terribly."** Here, *basanizomenos* is translated as "suffering terribly." "Buffet" doesn't really work as well in this context. *"My servant is home being buffeted by an illness"* doesn't quite have the same punch (pun intended)! Later in that same chapter, Jesus encounters two men possessed by demons. **"What do you want with us, Son of God?"** they shout. **"Have you come here to torture us before the appointed time?"** (verse 29). Instead of using "buffet," the translators chose "torture."

Are you getting a fuller picture of what is happening in this storm? This ship is being pounded, tortured, and afflicted by the waves stirred up by powerful winds. Don't imagine gentle waves lapping the side of the boat. This is all-out war – and the water is winning.

Jesus has concluded His conversation with His Father on the mountainside and decides to rejoin His students. This is no casual stroll the Lord is going to take. He must walk several miles out onto the lake, through treacherous waves and a fierce tempest.

Now the time is somewhere between 3:00 and 6:00 a.m. Matthew and Mark both note that it is before dawn (Matthew 14:25 and Mark 6:48), meaning it is before the first appearance of daylight. So it is dark; there are no street lamps on shore, and no lighthouses to provide guidance. And chances are good that if the storm was more than just a wind storm, then rain clouds are blocking out any illumination from the stars or moon. Visibility is almost zero.

How's the painting in your imagination coming along? Let's review the details so far. Utter blackness surrounds them. Huge waves pummel and toss the boat. The wind is so strong that no matter how hard the disciples try to row, they are unable to make any progress. They are three and a half miles from shore, removing any possibility of swimming to safety. And most importantly, Jesus is not with them. They've already weathered one storm on the Sea of Galilee (Matthew 8:23-27), but in that instance the Lord of the Sea was there to speak peace and provide security. This time, they are alone, left to fend for themselves.

I wonder if someone made that observation on the boat. I can just imagine Thaddaeus saying, *"Where's Jesus when you need Him?"* or James crying out in despair, *"Why doesn't He care about what's happening to us?"* Do we ever find ourselves asking those questions in moments of turmoil? In my own personal times of desperation, I have yelled out stronger pleas to my Lord – and in less life-threatening situations.

But wait! At last, here comes Jesus. He's finally made it to the boat. Since this is in the middle of the lake, dismiss any notion that he could have been walking on rocks just below the surface. And since we're putting silly notions away, please don't paint Jesus with a soft glow. He didn't glow! When Judas agreed to betray his Master, the men who came to arrest Jesus asked Judas for a sign to know that they were arresting the right man (Mark 14:43-44). Judas didn't point to Jesus and say, *"Why, it's the glowing guy, of course! Can't you see the white light emanating from Him?"*

So non-glowing, soaked-to-the-bone, hair-plastered-to-His-face Jesus comes walking by the battered boat during this massive storm.

I would have hated to be the first disciple to see Him. Do you mention this to the other guys? If so, then what do you say? These poor, frightened disciples have no idea that it is Jesus. They never expected Him to feed thousands, so why should they expect Him to walk on water? They are completely fatigued, pulling at the oars, frantically bailing out water, and fearing for their lives, when a figure calmly walks by their boat in the dark hours of the morning. I can imagine the dialogue that might have followed.

> *"Peter! Did you see that? I think I just saw someone walk by the boat!"*

*"What? Are you crazy? Shut up and keep rowing!
Keep your paranoid delusions to yourself!"*

*"Hey, Thomas! Look! Do you think that may be
Jesus?"*

"Naw... I doubt it."

I know, I know – realistically this conversation could have
never happened. With the wind blowing and the waves
crashing, I doubt that they would have been able to hear each
other in the first place. And who's going to stop to talk when
they are fearing for their lives?

And that fear is very real. The disciples were already in grave
danger, and then they see what they believe to be a ghost
walking by their boat! This detail is so important that all three
writers say the disciples were "terrified" or "frightened." This
fear is often overlooked in the story because we already know
the positive ending that is yet to come. But for the disciples,
this ghostly appearance would probably signal to them that
their lives were about to end. And in that moment, words
escape them and they are completely gripped by fear.

But then Jesus speaks. Pay close attention here. He doesn't
calm the tempestuous wind or the buffeting waves. He
doesn't tell them which way to row. He doesn't even get in
the boat immediately.

"Take courage! It is I. Don't be afraid," He says (Matthew
14:27). And then He stands there, on the water, yet in the
waves. Darkness and death surround Him, but He doesn't
take action. He waits. He stands there calmly in the midst of
complete and utter chaos.

If you were one of the disciples on that boat, what would you have done at that moment?

Peter comes up with an unfathomable idea. He wants to walk out on the water, in the midst of the storm, and join Jesus!

Although the Bible doesn't record this, I can imagine that there was some protest made by the other disciples. It must have seemed like a very stupid – and very deadly – idea. Would you have allowed Peter to do this? I guess it all depends on how much Peter was liked by his fellow disciples. Maybe some of them would have helped push him out of the boat!

And to all this, I say, *"Way to go, Peter!"* You desire to be like your Master. You want to do what He does. Everyone else stayed in the boat. I know I certainly would have! Let's be honest here – would *you* have stepped out onto the raging sea? Remember, there are no lights, and no glowing Jesus. How do you even know that it's really Him? What if it is a ghost, luring you to certain death?

But Peter is no dummy. Before he steps out of the boat, he asks Jesus for some words to walk by: **"Lord, if it's you,"** Peter calls out, **"tell me to come to you on the water"** (Matthew 14:28). Good move. Now Peter can listen more closely to make sure it really is Jesus. Maybe he can even follow the sound of His voice as he walks across the fierce waves to his Lord's waiting arms.

Jesus answers him: **"Come"** (Matthew 14:29).

That's it? One word, and nothing more? It does accurately reflect what the Greek says: ἐλθε (*elthe*). Although Jesus would have spoken Aramaic, I can only believe that this short

Greek word is a fair representation of the brevity of Christ's response. But one little word is not going to do Peter much good in guiding him to Christ in the darkness that surrounds him. If it were me, I would have shouted *"Marco"* several times and then waited for a response from Jesus.

But Peter went anyway. One word – that's all he has to go on. One word spoken amidst the crashing waves, the howling wind, and the desperate cries of eleven other frightened men.

I admire Peter.

And off he goes, miraculously taking steps toward his Savior. He puts one foot in front of the other and demonstrates a faith we would like to say *we* have. But his bravery only lasted a few steps. Eventually, Peter takes a look around him and the courage that once propelled him forward vanishes, causing him to stop in his tracks and begin to sink.

And what was it that Peter saw that caused him to start dropping like a stone? Most people believe it was the waves that scared Peter. But when we look more closely at the text, we discover that it was actually the *wind* that frightened Peter. This has always puzzled me. I've never seen "scary wind" before. My friends in the Midwest assure me that they have seen such a turbulent wind before a tornado hits, but I still wonder what it was that Peter *actually* saw. Although I am only speculating at this point, I tend to believe that this was no accidental storm. The timing, the power, the destructive waves all lead me to consider that this storm was induced by Satan – and perhaps it was this spiritual power that Peter gazed upon. Now, that makes a little more sense. Peter sees the forces behind the storm and starts sinking into the sea.

"Lord, save me!" Peter cries out in horror, fearing for his life (Matthew 14:30).

The next word is one of the most beautiful words in this entire passage – *immediately*. Verse 31 tells us that **"Immediately Jesus reached out his hand and caught him"** – not after a few seconds, or when Peter's face was beneath the water, but immediately. I am in awe that such a simple prayer would receive such an incredible response! We can all learn a lesson from Peter in how to cry out to God. Peter doesn't start swimming and holding his breath, trying to rescue himself from a force much greater than his own. Instead he uses his strength to do what all of us should do whenever we are faced with desperate circumstances. We should cry out, *"Lord, save me!"*

Jesus' response after catching Peter is one that has troubled me for years – and, in my opinion, has caused many incorrect applications to be made. Jesus tells Peter that he has such little faith and asks him why he doubts. When I was growing up, I always heard pastors explain that Jesus was scolding Peter for not completing the walk on the water. They told me that if he would have exhibited a bit more faith, Peter would have made it. When I would hear this, I began to believe that my faith was never going to be adequate. If Jesus tells Peter that *his* faith is lacking, what would he say about *my* faith? This also doesn't seem to fit with other sections of Scripture when people are commended by Jesus for faith actions that are nowhere near as spectacular as Peter walking on the water (cf. Luke 17:19, Matthew 8:10, Matthew 9:22, Mark 2:5).

Most pastors and commentators nowadays view this passage a little differently. When Jesus chides Peter for his little faith, it is not in reference to Peter's sinking but rather to Peter's doubt that Jesus had complete control over the situation.

Essentially, Jesus is asking Peter, *"Why would you doubt that I am able to save you? If you are sinking and about to be consumed by the problems around you, my hand will always be there to catch you. Don't ever believe that I am unaware of your circumstances or indifferent toward your situation."* Now that sounds more like it. And the application becomes much more relevant for us. When life is about to overwhelm you, and you wonder if Jesus even cares that you are about to go under, there is nothing to fear or doubt. He is right by your side, and nothing will be able to separate you from Christ Jesus, your Lord (cf. Romans 8:35-39).

Isn't this a magnificent story? Isn't the painting in your mind better than anything you imagined before?

Now go back to the illustrations you found on the Internet. Are there any that even come close? I couldn't find any. And it is in those inaccurate details that faulty applications are made.

Most have a glowing Jesus.
> *It's not that hard to step out onto the water with something lighting your way.*

Most seem to depict that it happened in the daytime with plenty of light.
> *It's not that hard to step out onto the water when you can clearly see where you're going.*

Most have non-existent waves, not so much as a whisper of wind, and Jesus dry as a bone.
> *It's not that hard to step out onto the water when there's no threat of being pummeled by waves and sinking to your death.*

Most aren't in the middle of the lake.
> *It's not that hard to step out onto the water when you still have the possibility of swimming to shore and saving yourself.*

Let our newly created illustration of Christ walking on the water be etched into your mind. Ask yourself, *"What does this new picture mean?"*

It means that we will sometimes find ourselves in the dead center of helplessness with no chance of rowing or swimming to safety.

It means that while we struggle in life, Jesus comes to us in His own time and often in unexpected ways.

It means that Jesus might be hard to spot while chaos swirls around us, but He is indeed there.

It means that sometimes He gives us one small word, and He wants us to come.

It means that His hand is closer than we can imagine, and that we never need to doubt that He will save us. ✝7

We pray: Lord of wind and waves, we praise You for Your incredible power and majesty. How often we forget that You control all things, and that there is nothing in the world as strong and mighty as You. Lord, forgive us when we see our problems as too big for You to handle. Forgive us when we believe You don't care about our struggle and suffering. Forgive us, too, for the times when we are too afraid to even step out of the boat. Thank You for Your incredible, saving love that has rescued us from the worries of this life. May we continue strongly in the faith, knowing that You are always with us. And when You ask us to come out on the water with You, and You give us one small word, may we step confidently, knowing that You've spoken and that Your hand will be there to catch us when we fall. To You be all honor and glory. Amen!

Pray Now!

The Amalekites came and attacked the Israelites at Rephidim. Moses said to Joshua, "Choose some of our men and go out to fight the Amalekites. Tomorrow I will stand on top of the hill with the staff of God in my hands."

So Joshua fought the Amalekites as Moses had ordered, and Moses, Aaron and Hur went to the top of the hill. As long as Moses held up his hands, the Israelites were winning, but whenever he lowered his hands, the Amalekites were winning. When Moses' hands grew tired, they took a stone and put it under him and he sat on it. Aaron and Hur held his hands up – one on one side, one on the other – so that his hands remained steady till sunset. So Joshua overcame the Amalekite army with the sword.

*Then the L*ORD *said to Moses, "Write this on a scroll as something to be remembered and make sure that Joshua hears it, because I will completely blot out the memory of Amalek from under heaven."*

*Moses built an altar and called it The L*ORD *is my Banner. He said, "For hands were lifted up to the throne of the L*ORD*. The L*ORD *will be at war against the Amalekites from generation to generation."*

(Exodus 17:8-16, NIV 1984)

I would like to eliminate a phrase from the vocabulary of every Christian. It would thrill me to no end if people could refrain from saying, *"I will pray for you."*

Now, please hear me out. I am not advocating that people should stop praying for one another! In fact, I am proposing just the opposite. My goal is to *increase* the amount of prayer and care given to the people around us, and I believe we can do so without merely *promising* that we will pray for them. I realized the power of this concept after reading this section of Exodus 17. This is an incredible story and one that can give us a great deal of encouragement in the area of prayer.

First, let's go back and establish the context of this account. A few short chapters ago, the Israelites were finally released from the cruel grip of Pharaoh. Moses marched up to the Egyptian ruler and cried out, *"Pharaoh, Pharaoh. Ooohhh baby, let my people go."* (I'm not sure if he was doing hand motions at this time, but I would like to think he did!) That took place in chapters 7-12. So the Israelites are now headed out toward Mount Sinai for the purpose of worshiping the LORD (Exodus 3:12). Along the way, the Israelites encounter many struggles. Some are a result of internal fighting and bickering, while other problems come from nations living in the area who are not too keen on seeing 600,000-plus slaves wandering through their neck of the woods. One of these groups was the Amalekites.

This was one nasty group of people. I like to call them the vultures of the day. They weren't known for their incredible victories in war, or their fairness in fighting. Rather, the Amalekites liked to pick off the weak, the old, and the sick. Moses recounts this in Deuteronomy 25:17-18 when he writes, **"Remember what the Amalekites did to you along the way when you came out of Egypt. When you were weary and worn out, they met you on your journey and attacked all who were lagging behind; they had no fear of God."** Like I said – vultures. It takes a special brand of evil to prey on the weak and elderly. Whenever I read this passage, images of bullies flash through my mind. I am delighted to learn that God was not pleased with this group's unfair fighting practices and lack of humanity.

Eventually, Moses and the people turn to face this cruel enemy and the battle lines are drawn. Close your eyes and imagine the following scenario. In one corner of the ring, we have the Israelite people. They have been slaves for hundreds of years and have few, if any, military-trained people among them. They are tired from walking and in need of some sustenance other than manna and quail. Admittedly, this group doesn't have much going for it – except for the important fact that God is on their side. Meanwhile, in the opposite corner, we have the Amalekites. They have no respect for their cousins (Genesis 36:12) and continue on in their wartime activities with Israel even after this event takes place (1 Samuel 15). And you can bet they had a standing army that would have no problem doing battle when they weren't picking off Israelite stragglers. Yet it is this very point that puts them at a disadvantage, because they are messing with God's chosen people.

We are unsure of how God communicated the plan, but Moses lays out the strategy that he will be up on top of a hill with his arms lifted high, while Joshua gets to swing the sword in the battle down below. It is in this story that we are first introduced to the young warrior who will eventually take leadership of the people after Moses is gone. His importance in this story foreshadows his importance to the nation as a whole. As you read this, you may be asking yourself: *"What exactly is Moses going to be doing while he has his hands in the air?"* If you guessed "praying," then you are absolutely correct! It is spelled out specifically in verse 16 but there are many other passages that speak of lifting one's hands in prayer:

Exodus 9:29 – **Moses replied, "When I have gone
out of the city, I will spread out my hands in
prayer to the LORD. The thunder will stop and
there will be no more hail, so you may know that
the earth is the LORD's."**

1 Kings 8:54 – **When Solomon had finished all
these prayers and supplications to the LORD, he
rose from before the altar of the LORD, where he
had been kneeling with his hands spread out
toward heaven.**

Psalm 141:2 – **May my prayer be set before you like
incense; may the lifting up of my hands be like the
evening sacrifice.**

1 Timothy 2:8 – **Therefore I want the men
everywhere to pray, lifting up holy hands without
anger or disputing.**

It is interesting that we are usually not taught to pray in this
position. We may see a pastor with hands held high in prayer
during the worship service, but for most people this position
is not advocated or practiced. From an early age, we are
taught to fold our hands, bow our heads, and close our eyes.
This posture is what most of us are comfortable with, whether
we are praying before a meal or bedtime.

But this is not how Moses is praying. His arms are raised high
in the air until victory comes. And in his hands is "the staff of
God." This staff had been used by Moses to enact the plagues
and to part the Red Sea. This symbol of God's constant protection and presence is now lifted high for all to see. Now, for
an 80-year-old man, this could prove to be a rather difficult
task. Actually, regardless of one's age, keeping your arms up

in the air longer than a few moments is not easy to do! Yet Moses keeps his hands lifted high in prayer to the LORD until the sun goes down. We also learn a wonderful lesson when we read that two other people assist Moses in this effort. There is no way that Moses can keep his arms in the air all day long, merely by his own strength – and those around him quickly realize it. Yet it is vital that his hands stay elevated, for whenever Moses lowers his arms from fatigue, the Israelites immediately start losing the battle. So to ensure his hands remain high in the air, a couple of people jump in to help. Aaron, Moses' brother, is the first one listed. Since he is the "mouthpiece of Moses" (Exodus 4:15-16), he is often close to his brother – in case there's something that needs to be communicated. If you see Moses, you can bet Aaron is close by.

And then we have this other guy – Hur. Other than a brief mention of his leadership capacity in Exodus 24:14, we know nothing else about him from the Biblical account. The Jewish historian Josephus records that Hur is the brother-in-law of Moses and Aaron (Antiquities of the Jews, Book 3, Chapter 2.3). I find it amazing that Hur will go down in history as the relatively unknown man who helped keep Moses' arms lifted high, securing a victory for the Israelite nation. Although we don't know much about this particular person, I've seen people like him all my life. Churches everywhere are filled with men and women just like Hur, who are willing to stay behind the scenes in support of Christian leaders. They receive no awards or recognition for the battles that have been won because of their selfless sacrifice. But they are glad to provide this service to God and others. 3

However, there is still one question that has always nagged me about this story. Why was Moses required to have his hands lifted up in order for Joshua and the army to be winning? Couldn't Moses just sit there quietly with his hands folded, his head bowed, and pray for Joshua and the battle below him? What purpose was served by having his hands raised all day long?

As I ponder this question, I remember Joshua. I am confident that before the battle began, Moses promised that he would be praying for Joshua and the Israelite army. Imagine Joshua down on the battlefield, swinging his sword and dispatching Amalekites left and right. How would he know that Moses was indeed still praying for him? If Joshua needed reassurance, all he had to do at any given moment was look upon the nearby hill, and he would see in the distance the outline of a man with his arms thrust toward heaven. Even in the thick of battle, one quick glance would confirm that the power of God was with them. Moses continued to hold Joshua and his army up to the LORD in prayer for the entire duration of the battle. In fact, the story highlights the importance of this aspect of warfare. Joshua's victory on the physical battlefield was completely dependent on the spiritual battle being waged by Moses and those who held his hands high. What an incredibly powerful reminder that someone was praying for them!

Wouldn't it be great if we could offer to others the immediate assurance of prayer on their behalf?

In my line of work, this is a common scenario: Someone comes up to me knowing that I am a pastor, and starts sharing with me their problems and difficulties. Hidden in this emotional outpouring is a desperate cry in the hope that someone will care for them. How grateful I am to be a part of people's lives at their most vulnerable moments! But along with gratitude come feelings of helplessness and frustration, for many times I am unable to do anything tangible to ease their pain and suffering. It is in those times that I am able to provide some comfort by saying, *"I will pray for you."*

These five little words can trap even the best of intentions. Too many times I have offered to pray for someone, just to have that promise flee my mind the moment I walk away. Has this ever happened to you? Have you promised to pray for someone, only to forget moments later? I applaud all those people who are either gifted enough to remember, or clever enough to carry a notepad with them to write down prayer requests. Later, when I try to remember people in prayer, I often throw out a general plea for God to be with all those I promised to pray for. Even worse, there are times when I see those people a week later, and as they are walking up to me I remember my shallow promise – then I quickly say in my mind, *"Lord, please be with Joe. Amen."* Then I feel a little less guilty saying, *"Hey Joe... I've been praying for you."* But honestly, I feel terrible when I forget to pray for someone. I am ashamed that I didn't support this person properly in prayer, even though I had assured them I would.

I'm afraid that all too often, the offer to pray for someone has become a polite way of saying, *"Wow, I'm really sorry you are going through all of this, but there is absolutely nothing I can do to help you."* So we throw out our offer to remember them in our prayers, and *voila* – we instantly appear helpful. What can we do instead that would *truly* provide immediate spiritual support and reassurance of God's presence? How can we, like Moses, symbolically raise our hands in prayer so others will know with all certainty that they are being prayed for?

The answer is not merely to promise to pray for them, but rather to pray for them *right now*. So when Joe shares with you his heartbreaking story of losing his job or struggling with his marriage, simply say, *"Joe, I want to pray for you right now."* And then pray aloud. In fact, this was the challenge I gave to my church members one Sunday: *Don't just promise to pray for others; instead, take the time to pray for them immediately, and in their presence.* What a privilege we've been given to join in the battles of life through the powerful gift of prayer! And why wait? What is the point of telling someone that you will pray for them later, when they really need the benefits of those prayers right now? Praying immediately demonstrates to someone who's hurting that you want them to have the blessing of God's presence and peace *at that exact moment,* in the midst of their pain. Now don't get me wrong – by encouraging you to pray for someone right there on the spot, I'm not implying that there is no longer any necessity to continue lifting them up in prayer in the future. You should certainly pray later as well. But more urgently, you should pray now!

Let me tell you a story of a young lady in my congregation who took my challenge to heart. She told me how she was out walking in her neighborhood one night, enjoying the wonderful California weather, when she heard a noise coming from some nearby bushes. She quickly realized that someone was crying. She glanced up and remembered that this was the house where all the trouble was happening. Often when she passed this house during her evening stroll, she would hear screaming and yelling coming from within. Based on its regularity, she knew that the family that lived there must be experiencing serious problems. And now, as she was walking by that same house, she realized that someone was huddled among the bushes, sobbing.

Her first instinct was to put her head down, cross the street, and keep walking. She thought about just continuing on down the road, and silently praying for that person. Besides, what else could she do? But then she realized, *"If I do that, how will this person even know that I am praying for them?"*

So she stopped beside the bushes and called out softly to see if the person was all right. She came upon the young mother of the house, whose tear-stained face quickly communicated that all was not well. The pain she was experiencing was evident as she began to tell my friend of the turmoil and chaos inside the house. The marriage was completely broken, and there was terrible animosity between her and her husband. After lending a listening ear to this young lady, my friend gathered her courage and asked, *"Can I pray for you right now?"* The young woman agreed.

And so my friend was able to lift her hands over this poor, broken woman and offer up words of prayer to God on her behalf. After the prayer was over, the tears had stopped flowing, and the woman felt more at peace. What an amazing opportunity for a caring Christian to raise her hands in prayer over someone in need! This kind of intercession gives both individuals the privilege of experiencing that prayer is not merely a promise to be fulfilled later, but also a comforting reassurance of God's love and presence, right here and now. ✝ [5]

Later on, my friend shared with me how much easier it was to pray for someone immediately. Initially, she was hesitant to try it, because she had never really done anything like this before. But after that initial experience, she went on to do it in other areas of her life. To her surprise, it changed so many situations from being tense and uncomfortable to peaceful and Godly, because prayer had become a more integral part of her life. It quickly became something that was not just a blessing for the people she was praying for, but it actually changed *her* life as well.

Powerful!

Since this was something I was asking my congregation to do, I thought it best to actually try it out myself. I have a neighbor whom I had become acquainted with when our kids played on the same Little League team. I ran into him one day walking down the street. He was visibly distraught and it appeared that he had been crying. I walked over to him and he proceeded to pour forth all his problems and concerns. I was happy to be there for him, and I listened intently to everything he had to say. By the end, I decided to try this "pray now" strategy. I asked if it would be okay for me to pray for him right then. He concurred, and as we stood there together in the middle of the road, I lifted his pain and frustrations up to the Lord. Just as Moses pleaded that Joshua would be triumphant in the battle, I begged God to give this man victory in his life and to provide the assurance of the Lord's presence in the midst of his struggles. And at that moment, there was no mistaking that there is a God and a neighbor who cares for him. As I've delved deeper into this type of prayer, God has appeared closer and more ingrained in my life. Everyday activities have become opportunities to grow stronger in my faith and deepen my relationship to the Lord. The command in 1 Thessalonians 5:17 to **"pray continually"** is no longer unattainable, but instead has become a motto.

I have often heard my wife pray for people while on the phone with them. After listening to teenagers and the pressures of their lives, she frequently prays aloud with those kids. So you have been forewarned – if you call my wife and share your struggles with her, be prepared to pray with her!

I encourage you to try this too. We all go through moments of crisis and stress, and we all need the reassurance that someone cares about us – and more importantly, that God loves us and cares about everything we are going through. The next time you are talking with someone who shares with you the difficulties they are facing in life, offer to pray for them right there on the spot!

Now, some of you might be worried about this. You start thinking about praying out loud, and your heart skips a beat and panic sets in. Don't be afraid to try this. There's something about praying aloud that scares many of us unnecessarily. Prayer actually has very little to do with the words that come out of our mouths. Rather, it is all about what is being communicated from our hearts. Trust that the Holy Spirit will be with you to give you the right words to say. Jesus gives a promise to us that is easily applied to this particular situation: **"Do not worry beforehand about what to say. Just say whatever is given you at the time, for it is not you speaking, but the Holy Spirit"** (Mark 13:11). Don't try to emulate your pastor or a favorite "prayer warrior" you know. It isn't about eloquence, or the number of words we say. Throughout Scripture, you will find some very short but powerful prayers. In fact, I am going to be so bold as to say that the shorter the prayer, the better! I base this idea on Jesus' own words in Matthew 6:7 – **"And when you pray, do not keep on babbling like pagans, for they think they will be heard because of their many words."** Keep it simple, and let the words come from your heart.

And when you do, you will be raising your hands over your friend – and that person will know beyond a shadow of a doubt that you care, because you took time to pray for them. And more importantly, they will be assured that God loves them more than they can imagine, and that He will be with them through every mountain and valley of life.

So don't just pray…

Pray now!

We pray: Lord Almighty, we are grateful that You allow us the privilege to talk with You. Your constant presence in our lives gives us great comfort, knowing that You remain ready to listen to our fears and worries. Forgive us for the times when we have offered shallow promises of prayer to others, and have failed to follow through. Give us the strength of Moses to lift our hands in prayer over our friends, neighbors, and family. May those around us receive assurance of the power of Your presence, and let them experience Your comfort as we pray aloud for them. In the name of our Lord, Jesus Christ. Amen.

The Worst Sermon Ever Preached

Then the word of the LORD came to Jonah a second time: "Go to the great city of Nineveh and proclaim to it the message I give you." Jonah obeyed the word of the LORD and went to Nineveh. Now Nineveh was a very important city – a visit required three days. On the first day, Jonah started into the city. He proclaimed: "Forty more days and Nineveh will be overturned." The Ninevites believed God. They declared a fast, and all of them, from the greatest to the least, put on sackcloth. When the news reached the king of Nineveh, he rose from his throne, took off his royal robes, covered himself with sackcloth and sat down in the dust.

Then he issued a proclamation in Nineveh: "By the decree of the king and his nobles: Do not let any man or beast, herd or flock, taste anything; do not let them eat or drink. But let man and beast be covered with sackcloth. Let everyone call urgently on God. Let them give up their evil ways and their violence. Who knows? God may yet relent and with compassion turn from his fierce anger so that we will not perish." When God saw what they did and how they turned from their evil ways, he had compassion and did not bring upon them the destruction he had threatened.

(Jonah 3:1-10, NIV 1984)

Have you ever felt at a loss for the right words to say in times of great spiritual significance?

Your friend is sharing with you her battles with depression and confesses that she believes that no one really cares about what she is going through. You search for the right words that will bring her comfort, and assure her that there is a God who loves her immensely. But your mouth and your brain have a communication problem, and in the end you are unsuccessful in putting your thoughts into coherent sentences. You worry that you've completely failed your friend and God.

Or perhaps someone approaches you with a spiritual question and asks about your faith and what it is you believe. With such an amazing opportunity, you hope to be as eloquent and persuasive as Billy Graham. But the only things that stumble out of your mouth are rambling phrases that you fear are unworthy of a person of your faith. You leave the conversation dumbfounded and wonder what it is you *do* believe in.

Now before you get too down on yourselves, remember that pastors are not immune to this issue as well. There have been many times in my preaching ministry when I have left the pulpit embarrassed by the words I have spoken, because I was unable to communicate what the Spirit was speaking to me through Scripture; the jumbled mess that came out wouldn't pass my first-year seminary preaching course.

I don't know why it is that we search for just the right words. I'm guessing that we have very pure motives for giving due honor to the task at hand, whether it be preaching from a pulpit or giving compassion to a hurting friend. Yet, we often worry so much about what we are going to say that we fail to communicate anything with real meaning.

You don't know how many times I've been completely discouraged after delivering a sermon or leading a Bible study and thought to myself, *"Why in the world would God choose a clod like me? I can't even put two thoughts together that make sense!"* I walk away, certain that God is about to bench me. I often wonder if it would just be better to keep my mouth shut. Perhaps saying nothing at all is better than saying something stupid.

At such a time, it would be beneficial for me to compare my awkward ramblings with *the* worst sermon that's ever been preached. Now, I'm sure most of us have heard some rather uninspiring, poorly-delivered sermons over the years. We've listened to some preachers drone on and on in a monotone voice, while others stagger their way through one incoherent thought after another. But I am convinced that none of these messages can compare to the atrocious sermon that Jonah speaks to the city of Nineveh in Jonah chapter 3.

We normally don't get as far as chapter 3 when we study Jonah. In fact, we barely get out of chapter 1 because that's where we find the amazing fish story that we enjoy so much. But there is more to the story of Jonah, so let's go back and take a closer look at this intriguing book. Before we begin, I invite you to open your Bible and read through the entire book of Jonah – which is only 4 short chapters (48 verses) in length. ✝[2]

We hear of a man who was tapped on the shoulder by God and instructed to speak a message to the evil people of Nineveh: **"Go to the great city of Nineveh and preach against it, because its wickedness has come up before me"** (Jonah 1:2). The uncooperative prophet balks and runs away, finding the first ship headed in the opposite direction. Why is he not interested in sharing God's love with the Ninevites?

We may wonder what Jonah's motives are at this point. We can speculate that because Nineveh is the capital city of the dreaded Assyrians (the sworn enemies of the Israelite nation) he might be scared that he will be captured and killed as an enemy of the state. Or maybe it could be that the foreign mission field really isn't his cup of tea. It is only when we get to chapter 4 that we see his real motivation for not following God's instructions.

So, for whatever reason, Jonah starts running. God had instructed Jonah to go east, but instead he heads west – far west. He hops aboard a ship heading to Tarshish, which many believe was located in the southern tip of Spain. It was the westernmost city of the known world at that time. Jonah was so vehemently opposed to carrying out God's command that he was literally trying to flee to the "ends of the earth!" He pays his fare, climbs aboard the ship, and starts to breathe a sigh of relief. His confidence grows with each hour that passes, knowing that there isn't anything God can do now to force him to go to Nineveh. But God makes it clear that no one can outrun Him. He sends a violent storm upon the sea that threatens the life of Jonah and everyone on board. The crew starts crying out, each to his own god. They begin to throw cargo over the side of the boat to lighten the load, in hopes of providing a greater chance of survival. Jonah, meanwhile, has slipped below deck to catch a little nappy poo. (Kind of reminds you of someone else who was sleeping while a terrible storm rages on – cf. Matthew 8:24.) The captain wakes Jonah and begs him to call on his God for help. You can imagine that this runaway prophet isn't too keen on that idea – the text doesn't mention that he prayed at all during this crisis. Jonah, at this point, is probably feeling ashamed. Deep down, he knows that his disobedience to God has created this dangerous situation. He has not only endangered his own life, but also those of the whole crew.

After casting lots to find out whose god has been cheesed off, the lot falls on Jonah and all the sailors become convinced that the storm is due to Jonah running from the LORD. They ask him what will calm the storm, because they are at a loss for what to do. Jonah "mans up" and tells the others that in order to save the ship and everyone on it, they need to toss him overboard.

Not wanting his death on their conscience, at first they try to row ashore. But the storm grows more and more fierce, and death is imminent. Finally, realizing that they are out of options, the shipmates say a quick prayer and toss Jonah over the side. Along comes a big fish, and GULP – there goes Jonah.

Although he is now in the strangest of circumstances, Jonah is alive! You have to admit that there isn't that much to do inside a fish. No TV and horrible cell phone reception prevent Jonah from catching the latest chariot races or playing *Words With Friends* on his Android™ phone. So Jonah does the right thing and spends time in prayer. He has plenty of time to reflect on his selfish rebellion as well as on God's incredible mercy. Covered in stomach acids and half-digested fish parts, Jonah cries out to the LORD. You really need to read the prayer (Jonah 2:1-9) to appreciate what is going on. For most of us, if we were stuck inside the gullet of a sea creature, we might end up bitter and angry at our situation. But Jonah praises God! After reading and re-reading that prayer, I came to the opinion that Jonah was actually dead before he was snatched up by the large fish and then brought back to life. Jonah speaks of the water sweeping over him and being tangled in seaweed, sinking to the roots of the mountains. As he sank lower and lower, I am convinced that he actually died. This fish was essentially his salvation as God brought him to life. Without this animal swallowing him up, Jonah would have been lost at the bottom of the ocean forever. (This also ties in nicely with the comment that Jesus made in Matthew 12:40 where he shares that Jonah was three days and three nights in the belly of a huge fish, so the Son of Man will be three days and three nights in the heart of the earth. Jesus died, and so I believe that Jonah did as well. And as God raised Jesus from the dead, so He also raised Jonah up and brought him back to life!)

†4

So, in chapter 2, Jonah is giving thanks to the LORD for saving his life as it ebbed away. And God hears his prayer! This is proof that it doesn't matter where we are or in what circumstances we find ourselves. We can be in the belly of a fish and God still knows exactly where we are and responds to all our requests. So if you find yourself in the darkest of places or the direst of circumstances, unsure if God is even aware of how lost you really are, remember that if God can rescue Jonah, then He can rescue you!

†5

God gives a command and the large beast vomits Jonah onto shore, alive and kicking. What an incredible tale! And it is at this point that we normally end reading the story. But if you take a look at your Bibles, you will see that we are only halfway done with this book. God isn't finished with Jonah yet!

Now that God has gotten Jonah's full attention, He repeats His command: **"Then the word of the LORD came to Jonah a second time: 'Go to the great city of Nineveh and proclaim to it the message I give you'"** (Jonah 3:1-2). I find it interesting that God repeats His initial directive to Jonah. How many times has God had to make multiple requests in my life, often with terrible situations interjected, in order for me to get the message and follow His instructions? Too many times! Jonah makes a wise decision and obeys God. I can appreciate that Jonah was much more receptive to that second order, based on what he had just gone through. We too, find ourselves more ready to follow God after He has rescued us. He has a way of opening our eyes and hearts to the things He wants us to understand.

With these recent events fresh in his mind, Jonah agrees to go to Nineveh. Stepping forth from the fish's belly and still smelling somewhat ripe, Jonah begins the 500-mile trek to the Assyrian capital. No details are given about the journey, which probably took Jonah about a month to complete. The text simply says that he went to Nineveh and specifies that it was an important city.

So how important was this city? Why is it labeled that way in the first place? The Hebrew word used in Jonah 3:3 for "important" is גְּדוֹלָה (*gedolah*). This word has several different connotations, all of which work well in this verse. One way to translate this word is to use the English word "large," in reference to physical size. Two verses that use the root *gedol* in this way are:

> 2 Chronicles 16:14 – **They buried him in the tomb that he had cut out for himself in the City of David. They laid him on a bier covered with spices and various blended perfumes, and they made a *huge* fire in his honor.**

> Deuteronomy 25:14 – **Do not have two differing measures in your house – one *large*, one small.**

More often, though, it has a connotation of being "great," whether in numbers or in significance.

> 1 Samuel 2:17 – **This sin of the young men was *very great* in the LORD's sight, for they were treating the LORD's offering with contempt.**

> 1 Samuel 4:10 – **So the Philistines fought, and the Israelites were defeated and every man fled to his tent. The slaughter was *very great*; Israel lost thirty thousand foot soldiers.**

It is easy to see that what is being expressed is that Nineveh has a large population, and therefore is a "great" city. This is further corroborated by Jonah 3:3 which informs us that the city is so expansive that a visit required three days. This is no small town we are talking about here! But there is another phrase in the Hebrew that most English translations fail to translate. I am completely at a loss for why it isn't included. After sharing that the city is *gedol*, the text adds the Hebrew compound word לֵאלֹהִים which means "to God." Putting it all together, we learn that Nineveh is a populous, important city *to God*.

For me, that makes all the difference in the world. If something (or someone) is significant to God, it should be significant to *me*. His mission is to be my mission. His mercy for people should be reflected in how I treat other people. We know that God **"wants all people to be saved and to come to a knowledge of the truth"** (1 Timothy 2:4). It is not up to us to pick and choose who we think is worthy of God's great love and mercy. Jonah had made the terrible mistake of dismissing Nineveh as unworthy, when it was "a very important city to God."

✝ 7

So Jonah begins this preaching task. As he walks down the street on the very first day, we finally get to hear the message for the people of Nineveh. And, in my opinion, it is the worst sermon ever preached.

"Forty more days and Nineveh will be overturned" (Jonah 3:4).

You have got to be kidding me – *that's it*? That is your spectacular message? Of all the things you could talk about, you choose those eight words to share (five words if you count them in the Hebrew)? Care to throw in a couple of humorous stories? Where's the three-point outline designed to change the hearts of your listeners? Do you have any PowerPoint® slides to go along with this compelling proclamation? Where is the connection to the culture and an understanding of the audience? Most importantly, where is the message of God's love for these people? Jonah needs to go back to seminary and learn how to deliver a proper sermon!

Now remember that God had already given to Jonah the exact message he was to proclaim (Jonah 3:2). I have a hard time believing that *this* was the extent of it! I have a sneaking suspicion that Jonah is butchering the words of God. His terrible speaking skills, his lack of developing appropriate content, and the complete absence of the love of God makes you wonder if his motives are pure and if he really does want to see the lives of these "enemies" change. He does nothing to persuade these people of the existence of the compassionate, forgiving God that he worships. He doesn't even lay out the sins of the people. Jonah is sulking down the street and doing the bare minimum that God is asking of him. ✝ 8

I am not impressed or inspired. If I was walking down the street and heard this fire-and-brimstone message being spoken by a wandering Jewish man, I would write him off as

a crazy person and be on my way. But you won't believe
what happens next. The strangest thing happens that ranks as
one of the top miracles in the Bible.

It actually works!

Jonah doesn't even make it three days with his dumb sermon
and **"the Ninevites believed God. They declared a fast, and
all of them, from the greatest to the least, put on
sackcloth"** (Jonah 3:5, NIV 1984). I can't believe it! How in
the world did that sorry excuse for a sermon have such a
powerful impact on an entire city – causing them all to repent
immediately and begin a fast?

The next three verses are just as remarkable:

> **When the news reached the king of Nineveh, he
> rose from his throne, took off his royal robes,
> covered himself with sackcloth and sat down in the
> dust. Then he issued a proclamation in Nineveh:
> "By the decree of the king and his nobles: Do not
> let any man or beast, herd or flock, taste anything;
> do not let them eat or drink. But let man and beast
> be covered with sackcloth. Let everyone call
> urgently on God. Let them give up their evil ways
> and their violence. Who knows? God may yet
> relent and with compassion turn from his fierce
> anger so that we will not perish"** (Jonah 3:6-9, NIV
> 1984).

The king is so moved and feels so strongly that he expects
full participation from everyone and everything! Even the
animals are to wear sackcloth, demonstrating their participation in the sorrow over sin! This repentance was not merely
a halfhearted, outward "show" – it was a full and complete

confession of wrongdoing that is equally matched by extreme demonstrations of contrition.

How in the world does a pagan king and sworn enemy of Israel end up setting a decree for everyone to end their sinful ways? This is clearly a miracle. And to make a great story even better, God heard the cry of these people and saw the repentance in their heart, and so relented from bringing destruction. It almost makes you want to break out the champagne in celebration. What a tremendous victory for God, and how wonderful that Jonah was able to participate in accomplishing this great feat!

At this point, you would expect Jonah to be doing cartwheels at the "success" he had in bringing about the conversion of an entire city. But Jonah doesn't see it that way. As we head into chapter 4, we finally learn the reason why Jonah was so reluctant to go to Nineveh in the first place:

> **But Jonah was greatly displeased and became angry. He prayed to the LORD, "O LORD, is this not what I said when I was still at home? That is why I was so quick to flee to Tarshish. I knew that you are a gracious and compassionate God, slow to anger and abounding in love, a God who relents from sending calamity. Now, O LORD, take away my life, for it is better for me to die than to live"** (Jonah 4:1-3, NIV 1984).

Can you believe this cry baby? What an ungrateful evangelist! He admits to God that he never wanted to do this preaching gig because he knew how kind God is, and that He was going to end up showing grace and compassion to all these wicked people. I really don't get this guy. If I was told by God to walk through my town with a message of hope and salvation, and I obeyed Him with the miraculous result of converting the entire population, including the mayor, and they all turned to God and worshiped Him, I would like to believe that I would rejoice in their repentance! It would be party time! I would be amazed that God could accomplish this incredible feat through someone like me.

But this isn't the reaction that Jonah has. Sulking, Jonah sits under a tree and believes that life isn't worth living anymore (chapter 4). It gets so bad that Jonah actually asks God to kill him right there on the spot (verse 3). From a statistical point of view, Jonah was the most successful of all the prophets and yet he never wanted his (or God's) message to work. Jonah is actually so upset by God's mercy, that he would rather die than go through that experience again. But as I think about Jonah's poor attitude, I see that there is a little bit of Jonah inside all of us. We each have a selfish attitude where we have no problem crying for mercy for ourselves (like Jonah did in the belly of the fish) and receiving God's grace; but when it comes to the "evil people" around us, we would rather have God's wrath and judgment be poured out on them all. We wish mercy for us, and judgment for everyone else.

Despite Jonah's selfishness, God uses this knucklehead to bring His message to the people of Nineveh. In some miraculous way, God used Jonah's words to accomplish more than one could ever imagine.

And then I remember all the times when I feel my own words are inadequate.

You see, our words actually do work because God is behind them. And if God is able to use this reluctant prophet to bring about the salvation of an entire capital city, then He can use you, and He can use me. If God is able to overcome the motives in Jonah's heart that are anything but noble, then He can use my heart when I am sincerely trying to share God's love and comfort with someone. ₉

I admit that there have been several times when I believed I had just delivered one of the worst sermons in the world. But many of those times, people came up to me to share what a tremendous impact the message had on their lives. Even when I felt my words were falling on the path, being snatched up by the enemy, they were actually landing on good soil and producing a harvest (cf. Matthew 13:1-23). We forget that God is able to take all our words, even the ones that are stumbling, hesitant, and less than eloquent, to accomplish everything He wants (cf. Isaiah 55:11).

Here's a story that illustrates this point beautifully. Back when I was a new pastor at a large church, I was asked to lead a service for children on Christmas Eve. We wanted to create a worship experience that spoke to little ones about the true meaning of Christmas. Back then, *VeggieTales®* was an up-and-coming phenomenon that did a fantastic job of sharing Christian truths through talking vegetables. (Even writing that sounds ridiculous, but it's true.) So my wife and I decided to show the video *The Toy That Saved Christmas.* The message was clear. While some kids may believe that getting toys is the true meaning of Christmas, the day is to be a celebration of the birth of Jesus. *He* is the true meaning of Christmas. The kids watched intently as we played parts of the cartoon. Pausing at various spots, we talked with the children, reinforcing the points being made in the movie.

A good friend of mine was there with her kids that evening, and she was appalled that this was how we chose to do a Christmas Eve service. She shared with me later how upset and disturbed she was that this service and sermon would pass as acceptable. She sat through the service disgusted at the whole thing, eagerly awaiting its end. But as she drove home, her daughter started crying. This mom leaned over to her child and asked her what was wrong. The little girl shared that she had truly thought that Christmas was all about getting toys. But now she knew that Christmas was all about Jesus.

That silly sermon actually made a huge difference in the life of this little one.

Now this mother has a whole different attitude when she comes to church. She realizes that there might be times that the sermon "falls flat" for her. Maybe the pastor isn't speaking so eloquently, or his content is lacking. Perhaps she feels that she isn't learning anything new and she finds herself thinking, *"I've heard all of this stuff before."* When that happens, she simply prays that those words would reach the hearts of someone sitting there. She asks God to use the words of the sermon to affect their lives, and that this would be the moment when everything changes for them eternally. She also prays that God would reveal something new to her that she had never seen before. And instead of sulking around like Jonah, she celebrates that God's Word does not return without accomplishing all that it is intended to accomplish (cf. Isaiah 55:11).

So the next time you are fumbling over your words and trying to convey coherent thoughts in times of great spiritual importance, remember Jonah. You may not be the most articulate speaker. It might even seem that you aren't making any sense. But those words to that depressed friend, or the answer to that doubting skeptic, or that encouragement you speak to your neighbor, will accomplish all that God intends. Your words are better than that worst sermon ever preached. And if God is able to take such seemingly lousy words to bring about a spiritual revival, imagine what He can do with you.

We pray: To the Almighty and most compassionate Lord, we confess that we obsess over what words will be the best to say until we come dangerously close to not saying anything at all. Forgive us for thinking that it is all about our eloquence and choice of words. Forgive us when we place such heavy burdens on ourselves – thinking that it all depends on us. We often fail, Lord, in remembering that You are behind the words we say. We are so grateful and thankful that You used Jonah to bring about such amazing results. Without a doubt, You receive all the credit for the turning of an entire city. Help us, dear Lord, to trust more in Your power. Help us lean on Your ability to achieve what You want accomplished through our words. Take our humble sermons we preach to the people You've put in our lives, and may we watch in awe as You turn hearts toward You and bring mercy to a fallen and broken world. May we go boldly and confidently into the world, knowing that You are a gracious and loving God that is quick to bring mercy through our meager words. Thank You for using us to bring about Your glory. In Jesus' name we pray. Amen.

204

For Further Reflection

For Further Reflection –
The Greatest Bible Study Never Recorded

1. What are your feelings regarding the books of the Old Testament? Would you be able to summarize its message or explain major themes? Why do you feel this way?

2. Think of a time when you had to struggle with or "debate" your understandings of Biblical concepts? What was the final outcome of that struggling? When does healthy debate turn into something that is not productive or God-honoring?

3. As you imagine the body that Jesus has after His resurrection, what do you hope things will be like for you after this life is over? Why?

4. Have you ever felt all alone in a situation, only to look back later and see the fingerprints of God all over it? Why is it so often difficult to see the Lord working in our lives while in the midst of our pain?

5. Have you ever gone through parts of Scripture and rejected ideas or teachings that you didn't like? How can this "pick-and-choose" approach to God's Word be dangerous to our faith?

6. Have you ever felt excited about reading the Bible? Have you ever encountered a part of Scripture that you've read over and over before but somehow, upon another reading, it suddenly came alive? What made it change?

For Further Reflection –
Sleeping with the Frogs

1. Moses was prepared by God to be the leader of the Israelite exodus from Egypt. Do you think God might be preparing you for something significant?

2. Many people feel unproductive when they aren't "doing" something for God. Perhaps, it is at those times, that God is growing, shaping, or teaching you something. Are you in a season like that right now? If not, have there been times when God prepared you for something great?

3. Pharaoh showed tremendous resolve in not allowing the Israelites to leave. Have you ever found yourself being stubborn in the face of God's working in your life? What excuses did you use to defend your stubborn actions? Did you ultimately win?

4. Some people keep sin around in their lives like a pet. They feed it, nurture it, and watch it grow in their life. Do you have struggles with a "pet" sin? What guilt do you carry around as a result of it?

5. Have you ever found yourself stuck with a burden or sin that you can't seem to shake? Turn to 1 John 1:8-9 and read this passage aloud? How does this passage encourage us today? What sins does God *not* allow us to bring? Is it possible that He forgives *all* of our sins? Will God reject your confession?

6. Have you ever hesitated to put an end to the "frogs" in your life because of the mess you would be left with to clean up? Are you in that state right now?

7. Brainstorm resources you have used or have seen others use that can help in the eradication of "frogs" from your life.

8. One time, my son Jacob broke a window with his baseball. He was very worried and freaked out about whether or not he should tell me that he broke it. He thought of all the excuses he could make. Ultimately, this made him sick to his stomach. When he finally told me, he felt such relief and realized that I wasn't going to be as mad as he thought I was going to be. What he had to do to help me fix the window was so much less of a punishment that he ever thought he was going to get. Think of a time when you obsessed over how bad a situation was going to be if you confessed a sin, but how the outcome of confessing was not as you had originally thought. Compare the mess of cleaning up after the "frogs" with the pain and experience of living with the "frogs."

9. Sometimes, when people feel relief from the pain of their sinful choices or worldly circumstances, there is a temptation to fall back into those sins. Share a time when that has happened to you. Was there a bigger mess because of it? How strong was the guilt?

10. Encourage one another not to return to "sleeping with the frogs." Pray that the Holy Spirit would strengthen those around you to stay "frog-free."

For Further Reflection –
When You Don't Believe That Prayer
Actually Works

1. So, have you ever prayed a prayer that you honestly didn't believe would be answered? Why?

2. Have you ever prayed "earnestly," as the disciples or Jesus have done? What made those times more urgent? How do we normally pray?

3. If you were Peter, suffering the night in jail before your possible execution, what would you be doing? What can we learn from how he handles the situation?

4. Peter has a much different reaction to the presence of an angel than have others recorded to have encountered these heavenly beings. Why do you think Peter reacted that way? How would you react?

5. The fact that Peter was rescued from his circumstances can give great comfort to believers all over the world that God still wants to save His people today. Has God ever rescued you in some miraculous way? How is it similar or different to what happened here in the book of Acts?

6. The people gathered to pray for Peter must have finally experienced great joy in seeing their prayer request answered positively, and in such a dramatic fashion. Have you experienced a time when God gave you exactly what you asked for? How did you react?

For Further Reflection –
Athaliah: Nominated for the *Worst-Mother-of-the-Year* Award

1. Share a time when you've felt abandoned by God. How did that experience affect your faith?

2. Looking back on that instance of abandonment, are you able to see how God was working behind the scenes, unknown to you, in order to accomplish His will?

3. Read Romans 8:18-25. How would you define "hope?" Share with the group and develop a full explanation of this word based upon the events surrounding Athaliah and the experiences of your life.

4. Have you encountered an extended time of suffering? How did you "keep the faith" during those trying times? What encouragement did you receive that helped or hurt your situation?

5. Has God ever surprised you in the way He handled a problem in your life?

6. How does the statement: *"God is in control"* receive clarification through the story of Athaliah. Share examples from your own life where you've been reminded of that truth.

For Further Reflection –
When You *Don't* Have a Lot on Your Plate

1. If you had been a disciple of Jesus, how would you have reacted to His instructions to feed the crowd? Would you have sprung into action or sat to see what others would do first? Would you have spoken up? What would you say to Jesus?

2. Has God ever asked you to step out in faith and do something seemingly crazy? Share with the group the feelings you had when God asked you to do it? Did you follow through? Did it strengthen your faith?

3. What might God be asking of you today? Take a moment to pray silently and ask God to bring something to mind.

4. What do you feel you have to offer God? What skills and abilities do you have that could be used for God's glory? Does it invigorate you or discourage you when you think of what you have to offer?

5. What fears are preventing you from stepping out in faith with what you have? If comfortable, share this with the group. Brainstorm other ways that God might use the gifts of the people around you. Encourage one another that *nothing + God = endless possibilities.*

For Further Reflection –
David & Goliath
(for the Ultimate Fighting Championship)

1. What trials are you facing (or have you faced) where you can relate to the underdog story of David and Goliath?

2. "You come against me with sword and spear and javelin, but I come against you in the name of the LORD Almighty, the God of the armies of Israel, whom you have defied" (1 Samuel 17:45). Consider the faith communicated in that statement. On a scale of 1 to 10, where would you place your faith? Where do you want it to be?

3. Share a "Goliath" in your life. Describe a time when you felt hope and confidence in the strength and power of God in the face of such a giant.

4. Read John 10. How did David's defense of his sheep compare with what you read in John? What other similarities do you see between David and Jesus?

5. Ask yourself why the height, frame, and stature of David would make a difference in the application of this story. What lessons do we learn if David were large and strong versus being small and weak?

6. What is the danger of relying on our own wisdom, strengths, or natural abilities? What will be the consequences if we are consistently self-reliant?

7. List your own strengths and talents. Do you use them to bring glory to yourself or glory to the Lord? Have there been times when you have forgotten the Giver of all your gifts?

For Further Reflection –
Removing Rocks and Grave Clothes

1. Remember a time when you felt that it was better for you to do something on your own as opposed to involving other people. Think of all the ramifications. Was that the best way to handle it? Why or why not?

2. The feelings we all experience at the death of a loved one are powerful in nature. Think of a time when you were angry over the loss of someone close. Why did you feel this way? Could Jesus have also experienced those emotions for the same reasons?

3. Imagine you are having a discussion with some of your friends who are not Christian. What "rocks" do they have in front of them? What objections do they raise to defend why they do not believe the way you do? Have you been able to provide answers to the "boulders" they have in their lives?

4. Is there something you still struggle with when it comes to a "rock" that blocks your path to growing in your faith? Take a moment to find the answers through contacting your pastor or strong, Christian friend. Share with them what's bothering you.

5. Have you ever been guilty of being harsh or judgmental to someone who is new to the Christian faith? Have you ever been treated that way for something you still struggle with?

6. Think again of your friends who are not Christian. If they were to become a Christ-follower today, what kinds of issues would they still struggle with? How hard is it to be patient with those who just came to faith? How can you gently help them remove the grave clothes they still wear?

For Further Reflection –
The Blind Spot

1. Although it may be difficult to see your own short-comings (hence the phrase *Blind Spot*), are you able to recall things that close friends have shared with you about some issues you have in your life?

2. Read 2 Samuel 12. David was aware of his sin, but he lived as if he never committed it. This type of self-delusion can actually create a blind spot. Notice how David was quick to condemn, but was unable to apply that in his own life. What other Biblical characters can you think of who also exhibited blind spots in their lives? What lessons can we learn from them in how they handled the revelation of their issues?

3. Have you ever been guilty of being judgmental against other people and their parenting skills? Have you ever vowed that you wouldn't act in such a manner without understanding the whole situation or appreciating the circumstances that family is in? Have you ever been accused of bad parenting by someone who didn't take the time to understand the whole story?

4. Why do you think Samuel grew up as a godly, obedient child while Eli's sons grew up to be scoundrels? What factors account for the difference? Hannah's prayers and attention? Different disposition of the child? God's intervention? Did Eli treat them differently? Do you know of families where one child grew up very devout to the Lord and one went completely the other way?

5. Have you ever knowingly, or maybe even unknowingly, caused someone to sin? Take some time to go to God in confession and receive the assurance that your sins are forgiven.

6. Are there times when you honor your children more than the Lord because it benefits you in some way? How do you try to justify your actions? What lies do we often tell ourselves in order to stay in that particular sin?

7. Have you ever been in a situation where you have defended an obviously wrong position? Why is it so hard to see clearly when we are in the middle of our error?

8. Think of some people who are close to you and know you well. Then think of those who love you and only want what is best for you, and whose judgment your trust completely. Take the time this week to open up to that person for some "tough love." Share with them your goal of discovering your blind spots, and your desire to live a life that honors God in all ways. Spend some time in prayer asking God to give you the strength to listen and not defend, and the courage to go through with any corrective actions that need to be taken.

For Further Reflection – Shammah's Significance

1. Do you feel as though you know your purpose or what significance you have in life?

2. After reading how Moses "took a stand" against the barrier that stood between the people and God, would you say that there is a barrier between you and God? What specifically is that? Did someone else come and "confront" that problem and what ultimately did He accomplish?

3. Psalm 94:16 reads: **"Who will rise up for me against the wicked? Who will take a *stand* for me against evildoers?"** Satan often takes stands against us in confrontation. What is it that allows us to take a stand against him?

4. As you imagine Shammah taking his stand in that lentil field, who else benefited from his courageous act? Would Shammah have even realized the extent of the influence he had? Are there "small things" that we do that can end up impacting a greater audience than we could ever imagine?

5. Do you have a powerful testimony of God's action in your life? If you don't have a "powerful" testimony, then what small things has God accomplished in you that can be used for His purpose?

6. What difference might God be asking you to make in someone else's life? What specific things can you be doing that might appear small but could still be significant for someone you know? What's stopping you from moving forward?

7. *"I would dare say that more good can be done by 100 Shammahs taking their stand in a lentil field than one man slaying a giant."* Do you agree or disagree? Why?

For Further Reflection –
Careful, That First Step Is a Doozy!

1. Take a moment and do a search on images of this story. Do these images portray an accurate description of what happened? Why or why not?

2. What lessons do you remember learning about this story of Peter and Jesus walking on water? How had you painted the picture in your mind?

3. Have you ever had a time in your life similar to when the storm was destroying the boat and there seemed to be no hope of overcoming? Did you ever doubt that God was with you during those storms of life? What, if anything, gave you comfort or peace?

4. Put yourself in the place of the disciples on that boat. What would you have been doing? Would you have continued to row with all of your might? Would you have been enthralled to watch Peter swing his legs over the side of the boat in an attempt to walk on water? Would you have been praying? Would you have been Peter and actually risked your life?

5. Do you believe that this storm was induced by Satan? Why or why not? Read Job 1:12-22. Does this provide any further insight?

6. Have you, like Peter, ever cried out, *"Lord, save me!"* What happened?

7. Has Jesus asked you to *"come out onto the water"* with Him? What is preventing you from taking that first step? What thoughts, fears, and doubts run through your mind when you consider placing your full trust in Him?

For Further Reflection –
Pray Now!

1. Have you ever found yourself saying, *"I'll be praying for you?"* Did you actually remember to pray for them? How did you feel if you forgot?

2. Are you one who actually remembers to pray for people? Share some strategies that might help others remember to pray.

3. Moses was the leader of the group and the spiritual head. He had to make tough decisions, but led with prayer. Aaron was Moses' right hand man who uplifted his younger brother and was the mouthpiece that encouraged those around them. Hur is someone that is relatively unknown. He is a behind-the-scenes kind of guy who was happy holding up the arms of the leader. As you take a look at these three people in the story, who do you most identify with? Why?

4. What scares you the most about the "PRAY NOW" idea? Offer suggestions or encouragement that could help you and others overcome those fears.

5. Have you ever had someone "pray over you?" Describe what it was like hearing someone else praying for you out loud. Now read Matthew 18:20 and continue the discussion of why it is so powerful when someone prays for you. Discuss how this concept can give us strength and encourage us when we have the opportunity to do that for someone else.

6. Share a positive experience of when you prayed for a friend.

For Further Reflection –
The Worst Sermon Ever Preached

1. Have you ever found yourself in the situation of trying to share your faith or provide comfort to someone and the words seemed to fall flat? Is there a possibility that God could still use the words you said?

2. If you haven't already, take a moment and read through the entire book of Jonah. It is a short book and will help fill in further details to help in your understanding of this book.

3. Read Matthew 8:23-27. Compare this with Jonah's actions. What is different? What is the same?

4. Read Matthew 12:38-41. How is Jesus' death and resurrection like the story of Jonah inside the belly of the fish? Do you believe that Jonah died and was raised back to life based on the comparison with Matthew 12? Why or why not?

5. Have there been times when you felt as if God was unable to rescue you from your situation because it was so bad? Compare that time to Jonah sitting inside a large fish. What lessons do we learn about God's ability to save people after reading Jonah?

6. Is God asking (or telling) you to embark on a journey? Do you like it? Do you feel a bit like Jonah? Again, what do we learn about the ultimate outcome of God's instruction in our lives?

7. What is important to God? Make a list of what He values most. How many times do we dismiss these things and how often do we value the things that matter most to God?

8. Jonah was probably giving the smallest amount of effort possible when preaching to Ninevah. Have you ever found yourself doing the bare minimum when it comes to God's commands? Could God still use you with that attitude? What would happen if you gave your best?

9. How does the ultimate success of Jonah give us courage when we see an opportunity to speak God's Word to those in our lives? If given the chance to share your faith, what elements would you want people to know? What is the most important thing when it comes to sharing your faith? How is this different from the sermon Jonah preached?

Notes

Notes

Notes

Contact

Pastor Manning would love to hear from you! What was your experience with *Shaking Scripture*? Feel free to e-mail him at markmanning@shakingscripture.com.

Also from Tri-Pillar Publishing

tALKING PICTURES

*How to turn a trip to the
movies into a mission trip*

by Dr. Jacob Youmans
Foreword by Leonard Sweet

Movies and ministry? What's the story?

Movies are everywhere - at the theater, at home, on our computers, even in our pockets! Our culture's fascination with the power of movies brings us together in a shared experience. But did you ever think that watching the latest action-adventure flick with a friend could provide a truly unique opportunity to witness about your Christian faith? Talking Pictures examines the power of movies in our culture and explores effective ways in which we can use any movie as a way to start conversations about our Christian faith.

Dr. Jacob Youmans, a dynamic conference speaker, is Director of the DCE Program at Concordia University in Austin, Texas.

$14.95 – Order online at ww.tripillarpublishing.com

Powerful Love
An Introduction to Christianity

by Rev. Dr. Lloyd Strelow

You've got questions -
God's love provides the answers!

Powerful Love gets to the core of the essence of our Christian faith. The first chapter opens the window to God's love for each of us. It is through that window - guided by the Holy Spirit - that Christians see, believe, and live the rest of God's Word. Throughout Powerful Love, Pastor Strelow uses the inductive method, using our questions to lead us to search God's Word and find His answers for faith and life. Written as a basic guide to the Christian faith, Powerful Love also includes thoughtful study questions and an introductory guide.

Rev. Dr. Lloyd Strelow has served six congregations in Michigan and California, including Prince of Peace Lutheran Church (LCMS) in Hemet, CA, where one of his primary emphases was to teach the basics of the Christian faith to all who seek to know the Lord.

$14.95 – Order online at ww.tripillarpublishing.com

for ordinary people

by Rev. Heath Trampe

What's so special about being ordinary?

In a world which equates "ordinary" with "not good enough," Rev. Heath Trampe uses powerful examples from the Bible to prove that even ordinary people can accomplish amazing things. As you journey through these 12 stories of inspiration and hope, you'll discover that "ordinary" is a pretty amazing thing to be. This 214-page book includes Bible study questions for each chapter, with in-depth answers and commentary. It is ideal for both individual and group study.

INDIE 2010 NEXT GENERATION BOOK AWARDS FINALIST!

Reverend Heath Trampe graduated in May 2010 with a Masters of Divinity from Concordia Theological Seminary in Fort Wayne, Indiana. Heath is currently serving as Associate Pastor of St. Peter's Lutheran Church in Fort Wayne.

$14.95 – Order online at ww.tripillarpublishing.com

Abba Daddy Do

exploration s | in | child | like | faith

by Dr. Jacob Youmans

Join the adventure of childlike faith!

When you're a child, every day is an adventure! Each day you see and experience life for the very first time. Reclaim the wonder and excitement meant for followers of Jesus as we explore the gift of childlike faith. Jacob Youmans, father of two, walks us through 40 true-life stories, discovering the spiritual in the everyday moments of childhood. Complete with study questions and scriptural references, this book is perfect for the individual looking to grow and be challenged, as well as a family or Bible study group.

Dr. Jacob Youmans, a dynamic conference speaker, is Director of the DCE Program at Concordia University in Austin, Texas.

$14.95 – Order online at ww.tripillarpublishing.com

CPSIA information can be obtained at www.ICGtesting.com
Printed in the USA
LVOW071151140312

273048LV00002B/3/P